D1649191

WITHDRAWN

The Cave Book
By Emil Silvestru

Master
Books

First Printing: May 2008

Master Books
P.O. Box 726
Green Forest, AR 72638

Printed in China

Cover Design by Jeff Patty
Interior design by Bryan Miller

ISBN 10: 0-89051-496-8
ISBN 13: 978-0-89051-496-2
Library of Congress number: 2007939094

Please visit our website for other great titles:
www.masterbooks.net

DEDICATION

To Flory, my soul mate, wife, and caving partner for 28 years, and my daughters, Alexandra and Cora. Never did a greater team roam the darkness with more inner light and joyful hearts!

TABLE OF CONTENTS

ACKNOWLEDGMENTS

I owe a lot to all my friends who helped explore, survey, and photograph so many caves and to all those young lads I introduced to caving and who still remember me so far away in space and time. Many thanks to my first true caver friend in North America, Mike Liston, who introduced me to caves on this continent and helped me with pictures and comments for this book. Special thanks to Bryan Miller for the illustrations and friendly manner of dealing with a troglodyte while putting the following pages together.

CAPPADOCIA CAVES,
CAPPADOCIA TURKEY

ABOUT THE AUTHOR

Dr. Emil Silvestru PhD

Emil was born in Transylvania, Romania, where he started exploring caves at age 12. His passion for caves and mountains naturally led him to become a geologist. His first research papers on cave geology were published while he was still a student at the Faculty of Geology of the "Babe-Bolyai" University in Cluj, Romania, where he later obtained a PhD in the sedimentology of karst terrains.

After graduating, he spent seven years working as a prospecting and exploration geologist. In 1986, he joined the world's first speleological institute (founded in Cluj in 1920 — speleology is the science of caves) as a research scientist. In 1990, he became the director of that institute. He held that position until 1998 when he left all his secular positions and began touring the country's campuses to speak about creation, sponsored by overseas creation ministries. Prior to that, he also taught episodically as associate professor of karstology at his alma mater.

With its more than 12,000 surveyed caves and a long tradition in speleology, Romania offered Emil excellent conditions for research and pioneering work in the emerging interdisciplinary science of karstology. Together with his staff at the Emil Racovi Speleological Institute, he performed extended research in the areas of general karst geology, hydrogeology of karst terrains, hydrological hazards of ore exploitation in karst terrains, cave glaciology, and even designing show caves. His experience and intensive research work in this specialist area has made Emil an authority on the geology of caves. He was also actively involved in organizing international scientific meetings and was on the board of review for the proceedings of the International Conference on Theoretical and Applied Karstology.

Dr. Silvestru has published 26 research papers in peer-reviewed secular science journals and has written a chapter on dinosaurs for a secular science book. He has published 13 research papers in creationist publications and contributed a section of a creationist book on flood geology and the geologic column. He now works full time for Creation Ministries International in Canada as a writer, researcher, and speaker.

INTRODUCTION

Leaving the Tower of Babel to settle in other parts of the world

There is a landscape beneath the landscape. We know it as caves; scientists call it karst. A long, long time ago, some of our ancestors entered this "underland" with eyes full of fear, with hearts pounding with excitement, and with a genuine interest in discovering the mysteries and secrets hidden in the absolute darkness.

But it was probably their immediate need to find shelter from the rapidly cooling climate — the harbinger of the coming Ice Age — that drove most of them. And it was also deep inside some caves that they found mystical ritual hunting grounds and a place to bury their dead.

Just as the climate was rapidly deteriorating, so was their belief in the God who had saved their ancestors but destroyed the entire world with a global cataclysm we today call the biblical flood. The memory of the great ark that saved the eight people God found worth saving, together with the selected land animal kinds, was fading into the harsh realities of everyday life. That strange event near the Tower of Babel, when suddenly they found themselves speaking different languages, had affected them deeply. The separation by languages not only split the one population into many separate groups, but the once-global knowledge and craftsmanship was also split between many groups that could no longer properly communicate. Very quickly, various groups found themselves with the monopoly over one or several crafts/technologies, while other crafts were more or less lost for them, so that they had to start all over again, almost literally "reinventing the wheel." This effect was even more pronounced as they were rapidly dispersing over the newly formed continents, becoming isolated from other groups.

Close and real encounters with wild beasts and all sorts of enemies filled their days, while their knowledge of God was in most cases fragmentary because of the language confusion. So people soon forgot about the true Creator God and started believing in all sorts of gods dwelling in all sorts of places, some of them in caves. So in time, altars and various other sanctuaries were built in

caves. This is why the dawn of the new mankind was so deeply connected to caves in those areas where they were prevalent.

Throughout history, caves have continued to play a role in the lives of many humans. Nowadays, karstlands hold (within karst aquifers) huge amounts of top-quality drinking water. Worldwide, 25 percent of all drinking water comes from karst aquifers and it is estimated that by 2025 that ratio will increase to over 50 percent! Caves have today become places of adventure and subject to scientific investigation, as well as being major tourist attractions. You will learn about the history and geology of these caves in the following pages.

Some find convenient shelter in caves.

CHAPTER ONE

HUMANS AND CAVES — A LONG HISTORY

We do not know (there is no scriptural evidence) whether substantial caves existed before the Flood. If they did, they must have formed by different processes, since the very slow cave-forming processes we can see and measure today could have not created them in the relatively short time available. God may have created pre-Flood caves, of course.

In any case, whatever caves there were pre-Flood would have been destroyed in the global cataclysm. Thus, all of the caves existing today must have formed after most of the sediments had been deposited during the Flood. In fact, the fossils of creatures buried during Noah's flood can be seen lining the walls of many caves.

Secular history teaches that caves were the very first shelters that humans used, yet Genesis 4:17 clearly indicates that humans built cities at the dawn of human history — before the Flood. Later, some people used tents (Genesis 4:20). The word "cave" appears some 40 times in the Bible (depending on the version), in most cases as a hiding place, but also as a burial (and on one occasion as a dwelling) place. The first mention is in Genesis 19:30, referring to the cave in which Lot and his daughters dwelt. Thus, we know

Two examples of simple dwellings used after the Flood

HOW TO MAKE A STONE AXE

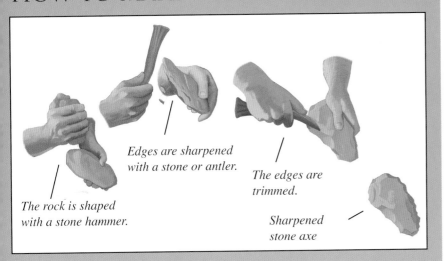

The rock is shaped with a stone hammer.

Edges are sharpened with a stone or antler.

The edges are trimmed.

Sharpened stone axe

that roughly 400 years after the Flood, caves were available to humans in the Middle East.

When they moved into caves, humans used them as shelters or as religious sanctuaries. One cave seldom played both roles — most probably because permanent habitation (especially continuous open fires) substantially affected those deeper parts of caves that would usually be chosen as religious sanctuaries. It is also possible that the belief systems involved did not allow the use of the same caves as habitat and sanctuary.

Many different human traces have been found in caves, from artifacts like tools (mostly made of stone and bone), pottery, and hearths to human bones. Many human footprints have also been found, usually preserved in still-soft clay. In a few cases, the sediment bearing the print has hardened, of which the completely petrified footprints in the cave Gheţarul de la Vârtop in Romania are the most outstanding example.

Human footprints are sometimes associated with, or even superimposed by, cave bear prints. One splendid yet little-known example comes from another Romanian cave — Ciurului Izbuc — where over 400 human footprints have been found and investigated. They belonged to a man, a woman, and a child who may have entered the cave to hunt the very cave bear that left the superimposing footprints. Although the

prints in this particular case are exceptional in terms of their number and the quality of their preservation, such traces are rather common. They reveal the fact that humans were in fierce competition for caves with other large contemporaneous cave dwellers.

The cave bear (*Ursus spelaeus*) was the most frequent such inhabitant. Sometimes the cave lion (*Felis spelaea*) and cave hyena (*Crocuta spelaea*) were also present alongside humans. While all three of these mammals disappeared by the end of the Pleistocene, humans, as we know, left caves to follow a different destiny.

The oldest tools found in caves appear to be the ones in Longgupo Cave in China, where stone artifacts were found next to "hominid" remains. These remains have been dated at 1.96 to 1.78 million years (Myr) by the use of many unproven assumptions. (More will be said about the methods of radiometric dating later, but let it be said at this point that this writer does not support any age that goes beyond 6,000 to 10,000 years into the past!) Many more recent tools and other artifacts have been discovered in caves worldwide.

Art associated with burial was found in Twin Rivers Cave, Zambia. It consists of pigments and paint-grinding tools and these are considered to be 200 to 350 thousand years (Kyr) old. The discoverers believe that the pigments were used both for body painting and for rituals, hence "people who were perhaps using symbols far earlier than we expected." This may well imply the use of a language.

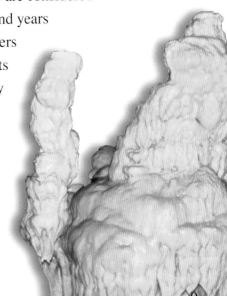

A) *Painting of wounded bison in cave of Altamira, Spain*

B. Engravings are usually made on soft limestone surfaces. In most cases they are found alongside paintings (they may in fact represent pre-painting "warm-ups" or even raw drafts of the real thing, as the frequent corrections or even erasures — in contrast with the paintings — suggest). In some cases they are superimposed on paintings, like in the above mentioned Chauvet Cave, usually revealing the loss of artistry and skills within subsequent generations. Of the many engravings I have seen, the ones of horses in the cave Isturiz-Oxochelaya (in the French Pyrenees) have impressed me the most, because of the powerful expression and the skillful use of the cave wall micro-relief.

C. The bas-reliefs are usually made of soft, pliable clay attached to the walls or even to large blocks. The most famous ones are the bear and feline figurines in Montespan Cave and the bison in Tuc d'Audoubert Cave, both in the French Pyrenees.

Finally, there are paintings in a number of caves and rock shelters that are believed to be non-religious. Probably the oldest among them are (at least for the time being) the painted slabs in Fumane Cave, near Verona in Italy. The animal and human figures depicted on these slabs have been dated between 32 and 36.5 Kyr.

Worship activities have also been revealed in many caves, especially as cave art. There are three different kinds of cave art recorded on cave (and rock shelter) walls and/or individual cobbles or slabs: (a) paintings, (b) engravings, and (c) bas-reliefs.

A. Paintings are either simple outlines (drawn with charcoal or mineral pigment) with no pigment fill, or true paintings with outlines, crafty charcoal shadings, and sometimes vivid pigment fills. The most revered and supreme among wall paintings are the ones in the Chauvet Cave in southern France. They have been radiocarbon dated at 32 to 35 Kyr. The artistry of the Chauvet Cave paintings is remarkable – not only the firm, almost one-stroke drawing technique, but also the amazing use of perspective and lighting. The artistry is even more admirable considering the precarious lighting conditions the artists had: tiny, flickering, animal-fat-burning, stone-carved lamps!

Lamps were simply stone bowls with wicks that hung over the edge.

How did stone age man create his paint?

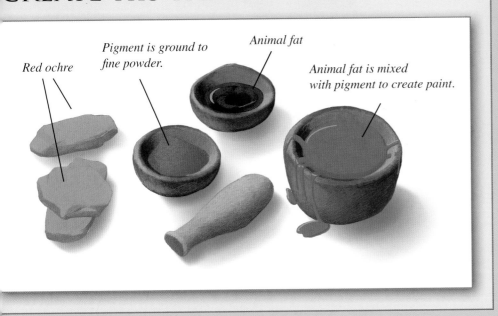

Red ochre

Pigment is ground to fine powder.

Animal fat

Animal fat is mixed with pigment to create paint.

Cave art and the age of speleothems

It is interesting to note that no cave formations (dripstones called speleothems — especially stalagmites and stalactites) have been reported thus far as part of cave art. It is almost certain that the artists (and especially the shamans who chose the locations) would have noticed the resemblance to animals in many of the cave formations. They likely would have seen this as a sign, omen, or invitation to use the speleothems in their art and acted accordingly. I see this as a strong argument that these structures formed after the artists left. I had the opportunity to see a number of caves in France in which new wall speleothems — flowstone — partly or completely covered ancient paintings. This became a serious conservation problem and triggered thorough scientific investigation in which I was involved for a short period. On the other hand, there is a

wealth of radiometric datings performed on speleothems in the close vicinity of cave art. Many of the alleged ages are much older than the ones attributed to cave art. I find it very difficult to believe that the experienced eyes of the ancient artists failed to identify any speleothem suitable for "artistic improvement." Yet, to my knowledge, no one has addressed this issue thus far. (A later section deals with additional arguments against long ages for speleothems.)

B) Engraving-graffiti from Twyfelfontein, the largest concentration of stone-age petroglyphs in Nambia

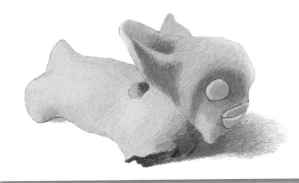

C) Illustration of bas-relief of a feline figurine

The Venus de Milo (Greece)

Coastal cave

RELIGIOUS SANCTUARIES OR THE FIRST ART GALLERIES?

When first discovered, cave paintings were considered to be recent artifacts, created by some eccentric character. As a better understanding of caves and their history was gained, they became widely recognized as early manifestations of the human intellect.

Although at some locations the intentional layout of animal bones (like four cave bear skulls positioned in the shape of a cross found in Peştera Rece Cave in Romania) clearly points to some kind of ritual, there is still no agreement among specialists as to the purpose of cave paintings, engravings, and bas-reliefs. Some consider them as elements of magic/religious cults while others believe they are simple artistic expressions at the dawn of human culture.[1]

In my view — which I share with quite a number of predecessors — there is little doubt that these complex representations are deeply rooted in religious beliefs. The small population of humans descended from the occupants of the ark had a clear system of beliefs from the beginning since their ancestor Noah "walked with God" (Genesis 6: 9). But as they spread out and lost contact with each other, their religious inheritance may well have started to dilute, with priority given to more direct and pressing issues, like survival by multiplication, which was still a divine commandment: "Be fruitful and multiply and fill the earth" (Genesis 9:1). If so, women and the mystery of conception and birth they embodied could have become one of the most important elements of their values. It is most probable that this is the reason why the earliest statues ever discovered — the so-called "Venuses" — represent women with strongly emphasized female features. Now, one may reasonably assume that plants and many ground-burrowing or cave-dwelling animals drew our ancestors' attention, especially as they grew more remote in time from their point of origin, toward the ultimate female (metaphorically speaking) — the earth itself — that they believed delivered them from her womb. In a way, we may see this as an attempt to forget the burden of Adam and Eve's sin, replacing God, the holy and just, with an unconditionally loving "Mother Earth." It was inside that same womb that the secret of all creatures' souls would be found. No wonder caves were associated with ritual entrances to "Mother Earth's" primordial womb. It may be that humans of the past believed that if they had the courage to penetrate deep enough, scratch, draw, paint, or model their main games' images, and ritually hunt them, the real hunting would be successful. Power would somehow be gained over those animals if their spirits were hunted first inside the sacred womb.

Evidence for this is provided by the bison in Tuc d'Audoubert Cave and the bear and felines in Montespan Cave, located deep inside those caves, in places accessible only through extensive crawling and even swimming. Furthermore, there are numerous human footprints around the bison representations, suggesting ritual dancing. The bear and felines in Montespan Cave are pocked with spear pits, an irrefutable evidence for ritual hunting. A great number of paintings in various caves depict animals with arrows and/or spears in their bodies as well as dying hunted animals.

always located very close to such points of resonance. When the cave walls do not have enough room for image paintings close to points of resonance, red spots are painted on the walls to mark the points instead. Conversely, there are significantly less paintings away from resonance points, even on walls with excellent painting conditions. It seems quite probable that chanting, dancing, and other types of ritual musical activities were associated with cave paintings, which reveals the rather sophisticated social and religious life of these so-called "cavemen."

Along the same line of reasoning, one must consider the recurrent presence of various representations of what appear to be masked humans, collectively termed "sorcerers" or "shamans" (most famous are the ones in the caves Trois Frères and Chauvet). Their presence alongside the most frequently hunted animals leaves little room for anything other than religious interpretations. As one may have already noticed, all

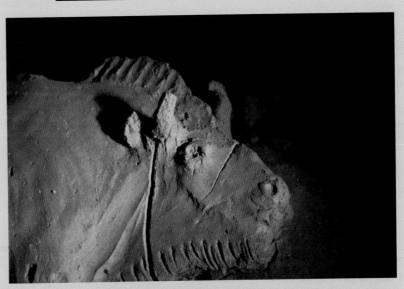

Detail of bison in Tuc d'Audoubert Cave

Cave paintings seem to have another interesting feature that is linked to acoustics. All cave rooms and larger passages have one or several points of resonance (i.e., locations where if certain musical notes are emitted, they will bounce back, amplified, from the walls). Studies in several caves in the Pyrenees have revealed that the largest number of paintings is

examples in this section come from European caves. And this raises an interesting question: Why is all cave art almost entirely restricted to Western Europe?

Europe has over 300 "decorated" (painted) caves (from Spain to the Urals), with the majority being found in France, Spain, and Italy. Some more

© Pierre Vauthey/Corbis

recent cave paintings, very few actually, have been found in Brazil, at a locale called Pedra Pintada (near the town of Monte Alegre) and are estimated to be at least 11 Kyr old. These paintings are completely different, very schematic, and have no apparent connection to either the style or purpose of the European ones. The numerous rock paintings in Australia, Africa, and North America are not taken into consideration here, not only because they are not cave paintings but also because they are considered much more recent than the cave art.

So why this restriction to Europe? Consider the clarifying question: "Why is Egyptian art almost exclusively confined to Egypt?" Now the answer is clear to any educated person: "Because it was created by Egyptians as part of their civilization." Here is the magic word: "civilization." Returning to the subject of cave art, one may confidently state that the paintings, engravings, and bas-reliefs in those European caves are the expression of an ancient European civilization. Certainly, this is not the picture mainstream anthropology and art history offers us! The concept of civilization is associated with the first sedentary, agricultural Neolithic peoples, and by accepting a Pleistocene (Paleolithic) civilization, the entire beautifully written and illustrated mainstream anthropology is seriously undermined. Man has evolved, we are told over and over again, and a civilization as early as the Paleolithic doesn't fit the evolutionary schedule. But it surely fits the Bible! Man was created by God in His own image and was very intelligent and skilled from the beginning. Only after the great dispersion of Babel did many human groups lose a lot of their knowledge, becoming more technologically "primitive." Take the case of the Chauvet Cave

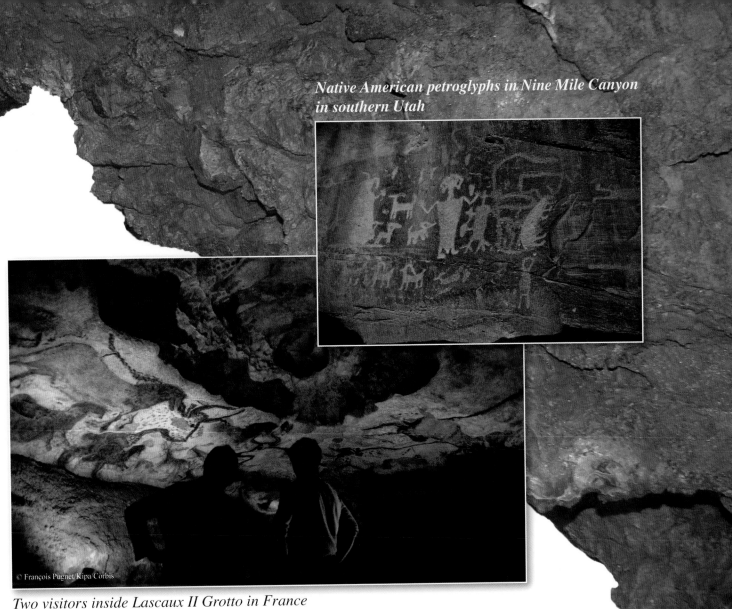

Native American petroglyphs in Nine Mile Canyon in southern Utah

© François Pugnet/Kipa/Corbis

Two visitors inside Lascaux II Grotto in France

paintings. When first investigated by specialists, their artistry convinced everybody they must be younger than the ones at Lascaux and Altamira, because they are more evolved. "Stylistic dating" was being used and that was unanimous until carbon dating "proved" them wrong. The Chauvet paintings are now believed to be twice as old as the ones at Lascaux and Altamira (which were already considered the pinnacle of "paleoart").

A serious conflict emerged from this: on one side stand the established and revered mainstream anthropologists, desperately holding to their evolutionary view of human culture, according to which art emerged at the end of the Paleolithic. (As somebody once said: "Archaeology is what the most powerful practitioners, usually professors, say it is."[2])

On the other side, there is a rapidly growing group of "taphonomists" (from the Greek word *taphos* meaning "death"; it refers to all the complex transformations artifacts in the archaeological record have undergone, including the subjective elements introduced by researchers and their biases when interpreting those artifacts). Theirs is a completely different — though still evolutionary — approach, based on techniques of "direct dating" which have yielded results that blow traditional archaeology apart. The ages they have revealed for long-established tenets of anthropology, for example, push the moment of the birth of art way back into the Middle Paleolithic.

The taphonomic approach not only assessed some rock art to be much older than believed but it also claimed, for example, that what was stylistically believed to be Paleolithic rock art at Coa, Portugal, was in fact less than three thousand years old!

Taphonomists believe that cave art could not have possibly been restricted only to southwestern Europe and that the lack of paintings in other European caves is due to the destructive processes of glaciation. As the massive ice cover was building up during the Ice Age, the overburden compressed the rocks in which caves are located and oftentimes the walls and ceilings would start to break down, sometimes completely, sometimes reshaping the voids until a balance was reached. Such an argument, however, is invalid because thousands of caves in Europe with similar-to-identical "art-inviting" morphologies have survived the Ice Age unharmed by breakdown and yet have no trace of cave art. Taphonomists further say there is no reason to believe that rock art was not widespread worldwide and was not limited only to caves, only that it did not survive outside caves because of much poorer conservation conditions.

In the taphonomic approach, spirituality seems to be completely ignored, cave and rock art being seen as a sort of popular entertainment! In my view, the primordial womb argument makes more sense and also provides an acceptable motivation for all this early yet elaborate form of art.

DID CAVEMEN EVOLVE?

Certainly! But not on the scale that evolutionists claim! There is no doubt that humans changed during the ages. They changed into different — sometimes worse — humans, but they were, are, and will always be humans. They did not evolve from apes, and many artifacts discovered in caves demonstrate this. But before we look at these artifacts, we need to have a look at what evolutionary scientists claim to be the history of ancient humanity.

The main criterion used to separate various human cultures of the past is the tools they made (or tool "industry"). Thus, at what is called the "dawn of humanity" (the Lower Paleolithic) we have the Oldowan industry (from the Olduvai Gorge site in Northern Tanzania). It is sometimes referred to as the "chopper-core" or "pebble-tool" industry. This is followed by the Acheulean industry (from the town of Saint-Acheul in northern France), whose most characteristic tool was the stone hand axe. During the Middle Paleolithic there is the Mousterian industry (from Le Moustier rock shelter in Dordogne, France), characterized by flint hand axes, scrapers, and points. The Upper Paleolithic had, according to evolutionary anthropology, brought into being

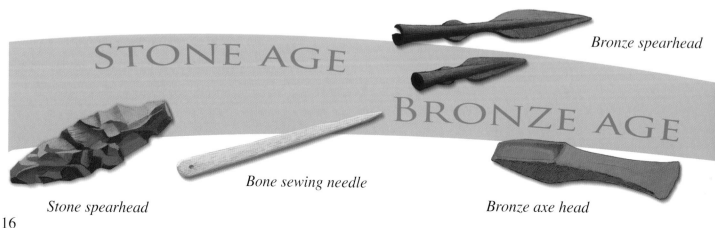

STONE AGE

BRONZE AGE

Bronze spearhead

Stone spearhead

Bone sewing needle

Bronze axe head

Humans were able to create sharper blades, barbed spear tips, needles for sewing, and fishhooks for fishing. Humans also invented new kinds of long-distance weapons, such as bow and arrows and spear throwers.

a number of different industries like Châtelperronian, Aurignacian, Gravetian, and Solutrean (all named after sites in France) toward the end of the Paleolithic, and into the Mesolithic (Middle Stone Age) another industry — the Azilian (from the cave Mas d'Azil in Southern France).

The humans that created the Oldowan and Acheulean industries are referred to as archaic *Homo sapiens*. The Mousterian industry belongs mostly to Neanderthals (*Homo sapiens neanderthalensis*) and the rest to the modern *Homo sapiens*. While these various tool industries undoubtedly prove a continuous progress, they do not prove any evolution from pre-humans to humans, only from less to more knowledgeable humans! There are other, more complex arguments that disprove pre-human-to-human evolution. The following is a list of human technologies and arts, their authors, and the characteristics revealed by these achievements. The age (according to evolutionary scientists) is in thousands of years. Even though wrong in absolute values, these ages still represent patterns through time. (See chart next page.)

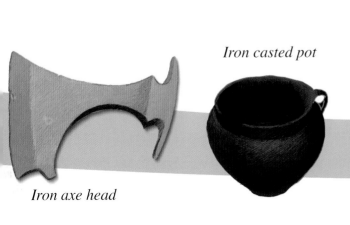

Iron casted pot

Iron axe head

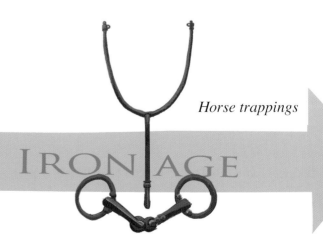

Horse trappings

IRON AGE

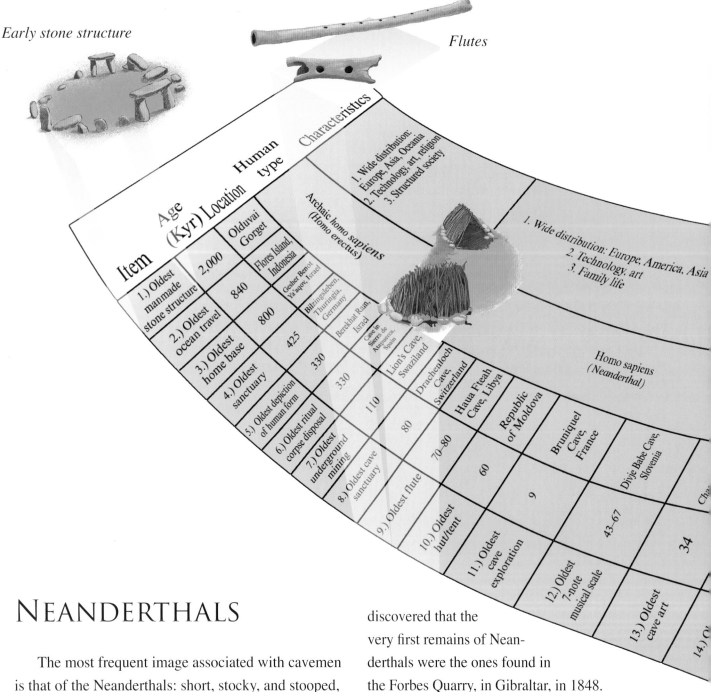

Early stone structure

Flutes

Item	Age (Kyr)	Location	Human type	Characteristics
1.) Oldest manmade stone structure	2,000	Olduvai Gorget	Archaic homo sapiens (Homo erectus)	1. Wide distribution: Europe, Asia, Oceania 2. Technology, art, religion 3. Structured society
2.) Oldest ocean travel	840	Flores Island, Indonesia		
3.) Oldest home base	800	Gesher Benot Ya'aqov, Israel		
4.) Oldest sanctuary	425	Bilzingsleben, Thuringia, Germany		
5.) Oldest depiction of human form	330	Berekhat Ram, Israel		
6.) Oldest ritual corpse disposal	330	Cave in Sierra de Atapuerca, Spain		
7.) Oldest underground mining	110	Lion's Cave, Swaziland	Homo sapiens (Neanderthal)	1. Wide distribution: Europe, America, Asia 2. Technology, art 3. Family life
8.) Oldest cave sanctuary	80	Drachenloch Cave, Switzerland		
9.) Oldest flute	70–80	Haua Fteah Cave, Libya		
10.) Oldest hut/tent	60	Republic of Moldova		
11.) Oldest cave exploration	9	Bruniquel Cave, France		
12.) Oldest 7-note musical scale	43–67	Divje Babe Cave, Slovenia		
13.) Oldest cave art	34	Cha...		
14.) O...				

NEANDERTHALS

The most frequent image associated with cavemen is that of the Neanderthals: short, stocky, and stooped, with sloping foreheads, heavy eyebrows, jutting faces, and bent knees. The first representative of this human type was officially discovered in 1856 in a cave in the Neander Valley ("Neander Thal" in German) near Düsseldorf, Germany. What were actually found were a skull cap, two femora, and other smaller bones from the arms, pelvic girdle, and rib fragments.

The 19th century German spelled the word "thal" — "valley" or "dale" — with a silent "h" which was dropped in modern German. Hence, there are two different spellings today: "Neanderthal" or "Neandertal." It was later discovered that the very first remains of Neanderthals were the ones found in the Forbes Quarry, in Gibraltar, in 1848. But at that time, this human type was not yet defined.

The German remains were interpreted in many different ways: belonging to an idiot, a hermit, or a medieval Mongolian warrior! By 1863, when the Irish anatomist William King coined the name "Neanderthal Man," the scientific world was desperately looking for fossils that would prove that Charles Darwin's recently published (1859) theory of evolution applied to the human species. In his *Descent of Man and Selection in Relation to Sex* published in 1871, Darwin actually

According to evolutionary views, this list goes back two million years before the present. Yet it is obvious that during that time the characteristics that define human society were present; humans have been humans from the very beginning, further adding weight to the biblical time-line of a six-day creation model.

Neanderthal

Eskimo

Fishhook

1. Wide distribution: Europe, America,
2. Technology, art
3. Family life

Modern Homo sapiens

Wooden wheel

Brno, Czech Republic	Rock shelter, Meadowcroft, PA	Czech Republic	Turkey	Slovenia	Knowth, Ireland	Ur, Iraq
25	19.6	14	9	5.3	5	4
Oldest woven basket	16.) Oldest fish hooks	17.) Oldest cloth	18.) Oldest wooden wheel	19.) Oldest map of the moon	20.) Oldest song	

mentions the Neanderthal skull. By that time, many scientists embraced the idea of humans evolving from apes and the Neanderthal man was considered the missing link between apes and humans.

Today, Neanderthals are seen as a human type (variety) derived from *Homo erectus*, a tall and slim human type. Their stocky, shorter body is interpreted as having been formed by adaptations to cold (similar to the Eskimo of today). Equally, their broad noses offered a larger surface to add a bit of moisture to the cold, dry air they were breathing in the proximity of the ice sheets that were covering large parts of Europe where they lived. On average, their cranial capacity (and the size of their brain) was slightly larger than that of modern humans.

There is still a lot of debate among evolutionary anthropologists about whether they are related to modern humans. Some

Neanderthals were often injured while hunting. They nursed their injured back to health.

actually interbred. Similar features were previously found in the skull of a child discovered in a rock shelter (Abrigo do Lagar Velho) in Portugal. If they interbred, Neanderthals and Cro-Magnons were members of the same species; that is less acceptable to the evolutionary mindset and this is why many reject it. Yet that accords with their descent from the four original couples that Noah's ark carried.

Spreading out after the event at the Tower of Babel, they adapted to the very different climate conditions that the Ice Age brought upon most of the earth. However, spreading and adapting often meant becoming separated from other human groups, and it was that separation that caused marked differences in the tool industries and general skills.

Neanderthals, for example, seem to have hardly used projectile weapons at all — except for javelins sometimes — preferring to use direct thrust even if that meant very close contact with fierce animals. Their superior body strength (compared to other human types) allowed them to still be efficient hunters, though they paid a high price for that. Some studies have shown that the most frequent injuries Neanderthals suffered were the same as the ones bull riders and other rodeo competitors today suffer. But unlike the popular image of brutish cavemen, Neanderthals did care for their injured companions. A famous cave in Iraq — Shanidar — has yielded a treasure trove of information about Neanderthal social life. For example, the skeleton of one male individual (dubbed Shanidar 1) revealed an incredible number of serious injuries

believe they are not, favoring the out-of-Africa origin of modern humans (Cro-Magnons, as they are called, after the location in France of the first Cro-Magnon remains described). These allegedly moved into Europe, coming from Africa around 40 Kyr before the present, displacing and eventually completely replacing Neanderthals. Other scientists believe Neanderthals — with a population never larger than several tens of thousands — were simply absorbed by the vaster Cro-Magnon population.

Some recent discoveries seem to confirm the latter view. In the cave Peştera cu Oase from Romania, the skull of a young male was discovered with undeniable hybrid features of modern humans and Neanderthals, which seems to prove Cro-Magnons and Neanderthals

which nevertheless did not cause his death. His right arm was withered, either as a result of a crushed arm or possibly since birth. His right leg was crippled and withered. One of the middle foot bones (metatarsals) on his right foot shows a healed fracture; the left eye socket shows clear signs of a massive blow that may have permanently blinded his left eye. All the injuries appear to have healed and the individual survived long after being injured.

In addition to all these, several skeletons from Shanidar show signs of severe ankle arthritis. All the above prove that the community inhabiting Shanidar Cave (and probably many others) cared for their injured, compassion being part of the Neanderthals' social patterns. Another discovery at Shanidar was the use of flowers to decorate a buried person, which indicates that Neanderthals had some type of spiritual life, too!

These facts point toward another important conclusion: Neanderthals had a spoken language. It is difficult to imagine such a complex social life without it. Yet some evolutionary scientists, desperately needing Neanderthals to fit their evolutionary models, still doubt whether Neanderthals actually spoke!

With a significant number of complete Neanderthal skulls available, we are able to reconstruct quite accurately the facial appearance of these ancient people. What one can notice is that some of those features are still present in some of our fellow humans. When such features emerge in modern humans they are called atavisms (i.e., evolutionary throwbacks). But that can mean only one thing: modern humans and Neanderthals share a common gene pool, being in fact one and the same species!

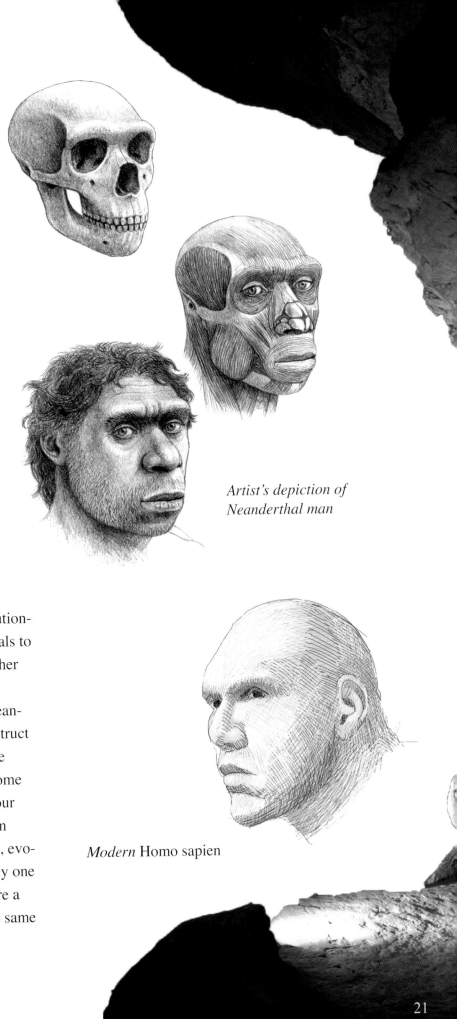

Artist's depiction of Neanderthal man

Modern Homo sapien

CHAPTER TWO

CAVES AND MYTHOLOGY

Caves are found in most myths and traditions around the world, even in places where cave habitation is not known to have occurred.

Egypt is one such civilization that, although it had little contact with caves (which are scarce in that part of the world), believed that the Nile had its source inside a cave from where the Nile god poured the waters out of two amphorae, a form of jars. A huge snake was coiled around the cave to protect these sources.

The Phoenicians believed that the god of rivers dwelt inside a cave. Eshmun, another of their gods (Adonis for the Greeks), had his sanctuary in front of a cave near the town of Afka. The river Nahr Ibrahim flows out of this cave, in which evidence for ritual (i.e., "religious") killing of a deer by Neanderthals was also found.

In the Assyro-Babylonian mythology of the Flood, the king Yimia is told by the supreme god Ahura to take one thousand men and one thousand women, pairs of each animal, and plants and retreat into a sealed cave in order to survive the flood brought by a demon.

Later, in the same area, the god Mithra was depicted performing the secret ritual sacrifices of bulls inside a cave.

In Afghanistan, the 10,000 grottoes of Bamiyan represent a true subterranean city. Legend holds that Vyassa wrote the famous Vedic poems inside one of them.

Caves have always been a part of Greek mythology and culture. Zeus was born in Lassiti Cave in Crete.

Relief sculpture of Ahura Mazda at Persepolis, the chief Zoroastrian diety stands on the Apadana at the ruins of Persepolis in Takht-I Jamschid

The lion of Nemeea (killed by Hercules) was hiding in a cave, and Orpheus entered the kingdom of the dead through a cave near Tanairon to claim his beloved wife Euridice from Hades.

The Romans have interacted with caves in different ways. The legate Crassus, by order of Julius Caesar, walled the entrances to the caves in which many of the fleeing inhabitants of southern Gaul, called Aquitanians, were hiding in 56 B.C.

On the other hand, the Romans believed that if, during their Lemuralia celebrations, one went to the mouth of a cave and spoke the magic words, *Mundus subterraneus patet* ("Open, subterranean world"), the shadows of the dead would come out and stay among the living for nine days.

Caves have also played a very important role in the mythologies of Central America, where they are found in very large numbers. In the Mayan sacred book *Popol Vuh*, caves are seen as openings to the Xibalba "Place of Fears" — the water-filled underworld. Xibalba played a crucial role in the Mayan myth of creation. Many caves in Central America are still visited regularly as places of worship.

In the Middle Ages, two of the very precious items used in alchemy came from caves. One was Nihilum Album (the "White Nothing"), which we call today "moonmilk" (a mass of extremely small crystals in a watery matrix). The other was Licorne Fossilis, consisting of the ground-up teeth of cave bears! Given their value, the suppliers made sure they populated caves (in the public imagination) with terrible monsters to keep competition away. No wonder caves were widely dreaded in those days!

Much of the saltpeter used to make gunpowder also came from caves. During the U.S. Civil War, for example, saltpeter was mined from Hamilton Cave in West Virginia.

In a sort of historical revenge, in the 14th century, a band of French knights (some from Aquitaine!) tried to conquer a cave in which the people of Piedmont in Italy (descendants of Rome) had taken refuge. Unsuccessful by the usual military means, they tragically resorted to an unmilitary method: they lit a huge fire at the entrance. The smoke killed 2,000 people who were hiding inside. Only a 14-year-old boy survived because he managed to find a little side passage that provided fresh air from the surface. When he heard about this, the leader of the French expeditionary force, the legendary knight Barron Bayard, had those who had ordered the fire hung.

In modern times, caves have been used for various purposes, from preparing cheese in France, Italy, and the Czech Republic to accommodating whole weapons factories (like the Michalova Cave in Bohemia, used by the Germans during World War II).

Most recently, caves gained public attention due to their use by the terrorists in Afghanistan (who unwittingly revealed their location by showing a small cave entrance in the background of the now famous footage with Bin Laden, which helped geologists locate the place).

The famous Dead Sea Scrolls were also found in a series of caves in the slopes of a creek called Wadi Qumran.

The Rodriguez fruit bat, often called a "flying fox," is only found in the wild on the island of Rodriguez in the the Indian Ocean. It almost became extinct by the mid-1970s as few as 70 pairs were left.

HOW DOES ECHOLOCATION WORK?

Bats send out sound waves. When the sound hits an object, an echo comes back. The bat can identify an object by the sound of its echo.

They can tell the shape and texture of a moth from its echo.

Bats are the most common troglophiles and many actually hibernate in caves. Not dangerous at all (despite many people's fears), these creatures are known for their impeccable sonar system that allows them to safely and precisely navigate through the absolute darkness. God has also arranged for these not-very-nice-looking little creatures to exhibit the "institution" of midwifery! Since females give birth hanging upside down high above the ground, there is a serious danger of the newborns falling to the ground and dying. Therefore, oftentimes one or two other females spread their wings underneath the delivering mother, ready to catch the little one if needed. God has also given bats other incredible traits. Some hibernating bats mate in the autumn, but the sperm remains dormant in the female as she goes into the hibernating state (a drastic reduction of the metabolic rate, with heartbeat and breathing slowing dramatically, and body temperature equalizing with the environment). Once she returns to active life in spring, the fertilization takes place. In some other hibernating bats, fertilization takes place immediately after mating but then the fertilized egg stops developing until the end of hibernation. Both these unusual characteristics have the same purpose: to ensure that birth occurs at the right moment so that the newborns have enough time to grow sufficiently strong to survive their first hibernation. One cannot but stop and wonder at how evolutionary mechanisms would generate such massive qualitative changes in the reproductive cycle of these creatures. A designed solution seems by far the best interpretation!

ave Olm (Proteus anquinus)

LIFE IN CAVES TODAY

There are many creatures still living in caves today. They are grouped in three categories: trogloxenes (Greek for "foreign to caves") which got there by accident and which try (often unsuccessfully) to leave the caves; troglophiles (Greek for "who like caves") which spend some parts of their life in caves like bats); and finally troglobites (Greek for "cave dwellers"), which live only in caves.

Various creatures end up in caves accidentally — most of them insects, sometimes salamanders, snakes, lizards, or even small mammals.

The vast majority of troglobites are arthropods (crustaceans, centipedes and millipedes, spiders, scorpions, and insects). Some live on land (cave floor, cave walls, and inside the vast network of cracks and joints), and some in the water.

The largest and most famous exception is the cave olm *(Proteus anguinus)*. When first accidentally discovered in 1689 (by Mr. Hoffman, the postman of a Slovenian town that was part of Austria at the time), it was greeted with the words, "O weh! Ein Drachen der Hölle!" ("Goodness me! A dragon from hell!") The famous Baron Valvasor, a chronicler of that part of Slovenia (called Carniolia at that time),

later referred to the animal. But the person who is credited with the scientific discovery – in fact, the first scientific description and classification — of this creature was the Viennese doctor and zoologist J.N. Laurenti, one hundred years later. The animal, an amphibian like newts and salamanders, has a serpent-like, white-pinkish body (discolored like all creatures living in perpetual darkness) up to 12 inches (30 cm) in length. It has four tiny legs like appendices and intensely red external gills. One of the strangest characteristics of this animal is the fact that it reaches sexual maturity in the larval stage (this is called neoteny and evolutionary science has no ready explanation for it). Its only known close relative is the mudpuppy *(Necturus maculosus)*, which, however, lives on the surface in rivers and weedy ponds.

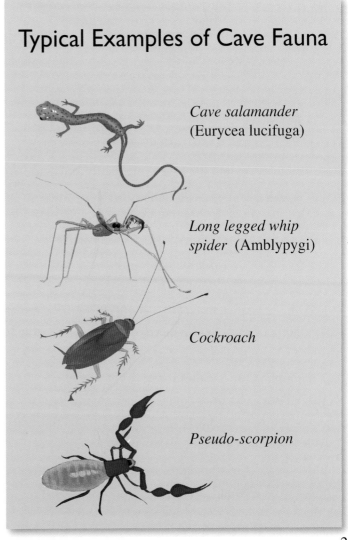

Typical Examples of Cave Fauna

Cave salamander (Eurycea lucifuga)

Long legged whip spider (Amblypygi)

Cockroach

Pseudo-scorpion

MOVILE CAVE (ROMANIA)

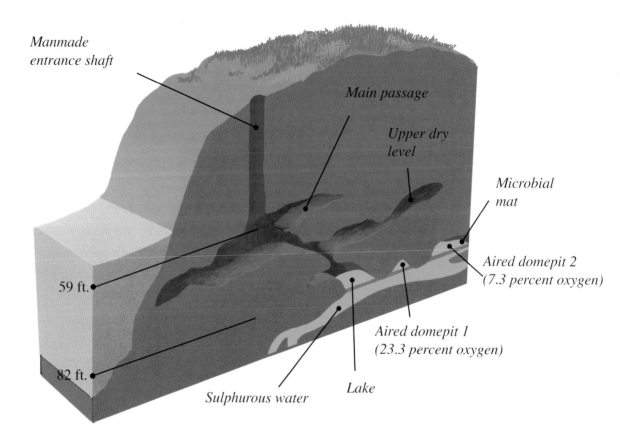

Manmade entrance shaft

Main passage

Upper dry level

Microbial mat

Aired domepit 2 (7.3 percent oxygen)

59 ft.

82 ft.

Aired domepit 1 (23.3 percent oxygen)

Sulphurous water

Lake

Many terrestrial cave arthropods have been found to travel through hundreds of feet of rock from the caves close to the surface in search of food. This is a clear indication that they were originally surface dwellers that discovered an empty niche that they promptly occupied. It is believed that they did this mainly under the pressure of the oncoming Ice Age, which made their normal habitat — the soil and the network of cracks and joints at the surface of the limestone — too harsh for life. The fact that they are still capable of making the journey to the surface today strongly suggests that their "invasion" of the underworld happened in a rather recent past. Since caves likely did not exist prior to the Flood, as previously discussed, it makes sense that cave dwellers today were not created to live in caves. Rather, their change of lifestyle must have occurred sometime in the 40+ centuries since Noah's flood.

One very spectacular cave environment was discovered in Movile Cave in Romania, close to the Black Sea. Sulfur-rich water rises from deep inside the rocks and reaches the cave, where it forms a number of subterranean lakes. Bacteria metabolize the sulfur, creating an inch-thick bacterial mat on the surface of the lakes. This "bacterial soup" is eaten by small arthropods, which in turn are the food for larger arthropods. Thirty-two new species and two new genera for science were discovered in this cave, from insects to millipedes and leeches. All these creatures thrive in this absolute darkness only because the bacteria do not need light, but chemicals (sulfur), to exist. Such chemotrophic food chains are also found on the bottom of the oceans around hot vents (so-called "black smokers"). Similar chemotrophic ecosystems have been found in other caves around the world, but the one at Movile is the first to be thoroughly investigated.

The cave attracted even exobiologists (biologists who search for extraterrestrial life) who believe that conditions like those in this cave may be found on other planets. It is much less expensive to study such ecosystems by descending 65 feet (20 m) under the ground than miles under the sea where hot vents are found!

Troglobite life (in caves) represents an extreme case of adaptation to a new environment, adaptation that came with clear loss of genetic information. The first to reach caves (probably via cracks, joints, and faults before even cave entrances opened) to become troglobites were likely small creatures like the arthropods. They would have easily and rapidly adapted to the new environment; natural selection would have tended to favor the ones who adapted "first and best." Basically all useful changes that occurred during the process of adaptation meant losing something they already had (like eyesight and/or color), or increasing existing appendages (like antennae). None of these sorts of changes represents an evolutionary step toward a new type of organism (i.e., adding new genetic information, increasing functional complexity). They represent, rather, a simplification and regression of an existing set of genomes (gene pool). The fact that many of the troglobitic arthropods have been found very close to the surface (where they travel along joints and cracks in search for food) is good evidence that they originally came from the surface and then adapted to the subterranean environment.

Other more complex troglobites, like the cave olm and the cave fish, also appear to have lost genetic information, becoming blind and colorless. Experiments have shown that if it is exposed to light, the olm starts developing pigmentation, something it already had before it moved to caves. So one cannot claim

HUMAN ISOLATION EXPERIMENTS

In 1938, two men spent 32 days inside a Kentucky cave in what may be the first such recorded experiment. In 1962, Michel Siffre (aged 23) spent two months in a cave in the Maritime Alps in France without any time cues. He repeated the experiment several times, the last time in 2000 (at age 61) for 73 days. Others have also run similar experiments of total isolation and the results have always been the same: the more time that is spent in isolation and dark, the longer the sleep-wake daily cycle gets. For example, some subjects could stay awake for 20 hours and sleep for 12 and be perfectly fine. This shows how important the natural cycle of light and darkness that God established for humans can be.

Unknown for many years, the longest recorded continuous stay in a cave was not an experiment but rather a life-saving experience. Thirty-eight Ukrainian Jews hid for nearly two years in the Priest's Grotto (Popowa Yama), a 77-mile-long gypsum cave labyrinth during World War II.

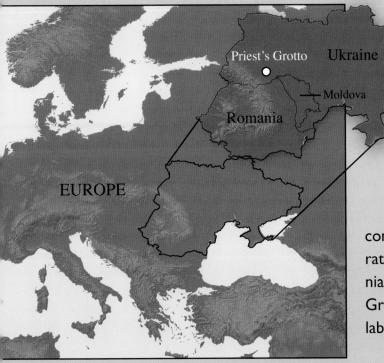

EUROPE

Romania

Moldova

Ukraine

Priest's Grotto

that troglobite life in any way proves evolution from goo-to-you! It proves, in fact, the opposite. Submitted to severe environmental stress, creatures can adapt by losing some of their original characteristics while extending other existing ones. Such loss will make a hypothetical next adaptation to radically different conditions more difficult because the genome has been depleted, so the chances are increased, of a species with such a new change going extinct. Such a trend is definitely opposed to the concept of evolving into a new, more complex species.

CAVE CLIMATE

If a cave is long/deep enough, it will inevitably develop its own climate. Being deep below the surface, a cave's atmosphere is much less influenced by the outer atmosphere. In most rocks, a 86°F (30°C) temperature fluctuation in the atmosphere above them is reduced to less than 33.8° F (1°C) at 22.44 inches (57 cm) below the surface. There are three types of cave microclimates (given the modest size of caves compared to the surface terrain, a Romanian scientist[3] proposed the term "meroclimate," which would be the equivalent of a micro-microclimate):

• **the disturbance microclimate**, present in the entrance area where the cave climate is drastically influenced by surface temperature fluctuations (the amplitude of the fluc-

tuation is over 50°F [10°C] in temperate climates);

• **the transitional microclimate**, beyond the disturbance microclimate, where the amplitude of fluctuations is less than 50°F (10°C) in temperate climates);

• **the stability microclimate**, in the deeper parts of the caves where the amplitude of fluctuations is below 33.8°F (1°C) (in temperate climates).

The temperature in the stability microclimate depends on two factors: the heat coming up from inside the earth (heat flow) and the temperature of the atmosphere above the surface of the terrain. The deeper the cave, the higher the influence of the heat flow; conversely, the closer to the surface the cave, the higher the influence of the outer atmosphere. In the vast majority of caves, the latter is the most important. The rock substrate tends to be in temperature equilibrium with the atmosphere, and because the rock has a

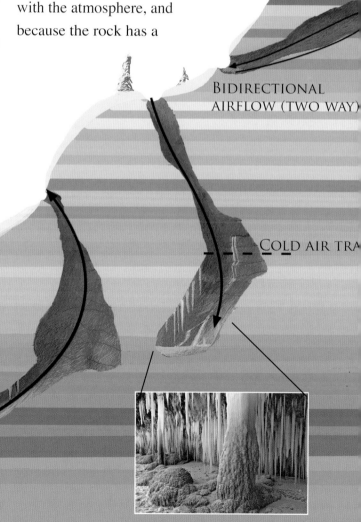

Cave climate illustration

UNIDIRECTIONAL AIRFLOW (ONE WAY)

BIDIRECTIONAL AIRFLOW (TWO WAY)

COLD AIR TRA

Ice Cave, Grand Island, Lake Superior, Michigan's Upper Peninsula, USA

significantly higher thermal inertia (it takes longer to cool or warm); its average temperature is very close to the multi-annual average temperature of the atmosphere in that geographic location. That is usually calculated by taking the average of each month, adding up at least ten consecutive years, and averaging that. The water contained in the caves (karst aquifers) tends to closely follow the same pattern, unless it rapidly transits caves (in which case it does not have the time to thermally balance with the surrounding rock). This is why karst water temperature can be an excellent indicator for the time the water has spent under the ground.

The humidity (air moisture) in caves is very high, usually above 90 percent, and it seldom fluctuates significantly.

The air in caves is rarely stagnant. There are two basic types of caves in regard to air circulation: unidirectional (one-way) and bidirectional (two-way). The former are caves with only one entrance (cul-de-sac) in which the air that warms in the deeper parts rises to the ceiling and moves toward the mouth of the cave, exiting in the upper part of it. Colder air flows in at the lower part of the entrance to replace the expelled air. The steeper the cave floor, the more intense the air current. In temperate climates, ice can accumulate in cul-de-sac shafts because they act as traps for cold air: cold air falls in during the winter, cooling the rock walls. In spring, when melting starts (and with it infiltration of meltwater) the temperature at the bottom of the shafts is still below freezing (and will remain so during most of the year because the rock sustains the cold), so the infiltrated water freezes and ice accumulates.

Bidirectional circulation caves (also known as blowing caves) always have at least two entrances, located at different elevations. In the winter, cold air penetrates through the lower opening, warms up inside the cave, and emerges through the upper opening. In the summer, the airflow direction changes; cold air flows out of the cave through the lower opening, and warm air from the surface is sucked in through the upper opening. When located at higher elevations, perennial ice can form in the lower sections of the cave, because cold air cools the rock walls that will sustain negative temperatures through most of the year. Such a cave is called a dynamic ice cave.

CAVES — THE HEALTH BENEFITS

An interesting characteristic of caves located deep under the surface is the abundance of negative ions in their air. The ions are charged particles that arise when atoms or molecules lose or gain an electron. Negative ions in the air are usually oxygen atoms that have gained an electron while positive ions are usually carbon dioxide molecules that have lost an electron. Ancient yoga masters recommended breathing exercises as being more effective near a waterfall or in a cave, or best near a waterfall inside a cave! The latter is the place with the largest number of negative ions and there is scientific evidence that negative ions can be beneficial to health.[4] This happens because of the thick rock ceiling, which cancels out most of the cosmic radiation (which is responsible for positive ionization of the atmosphere). A waterfall (free-falling water) produces large numbers of negative ions and the absence of cosmic radiation preserves them. Often, if people who enter caves with a cold or flu, and spend enough time underground, they will notice that their health improves significantly faster than on the surface. It happened to me frequently. Some caves in Europe have in fact been fitted for therapeutic purposes (speleotherapy).

CHAPTER THREE

CAVES AND KARST — SOME OF THE MORE TECHNICAL DETAILS

What is a cave? By international agreement, a cave is considered a natural opening in rocks, accessible to humans, which is longer than it is deep and is at least 33 feet (10 m) in length. When depth (vertical dimension) is greater than length and is at least 33 feet, the term used is natural well or open shaft (in North America), pot hole (in the United Kingdom), or aven (in France and Romania). Various natural processes can generate such openings in all sorts of rocks. However, the vast majority of caves were formed in a rather small group of rocks called karstic rocks. They cover approximately 12 percent of the ice-free landmass, with China having the largest surfaces (over 386,100 square miles or one million square kilometers, of which half are in one continuous surface!).

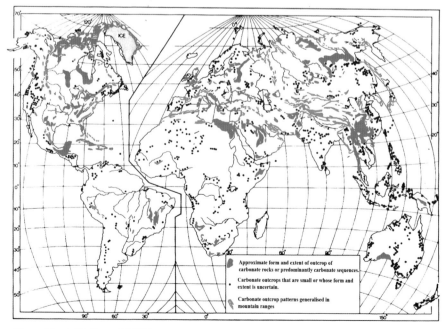

(From Ford, D.C. and Williams, P. *Karst Geomorphology and Hydrology;* Chapman & Hall, 1992; Chapter 1 - Introduction to Karst; p. 4; used with permission from Springer Science and Business Media)

KARSTIC ROCKS

All rocks are soluble, but some are much more soluble to natural acids that are present at the surface of the earth. Carbonic acid is the most abundant of these acids because rainwater enriched with carbon dioxide (mainly from the soil and the bacteria in it) becomes a mild carbonic acid (soda). Obviously, salts of the carbonic acid — carbonates — are the most readily dissolved by this acid through acid dissolution according to the following generic reaction:

$$CaCO_3 + H_2CO_3 \rightleftharpoons Ca^{2+} + 2HCO_3$$

Sedimentary carbonates are in fact a continuous range of mixtures of various minerals with impurities. Limestone is built mostly of calcium carbonate and is the easiest to dissolve. The mineral dolomite is a double carbonate of calcium and magnesium and it is believed to form by the addition of magnesium atoms to the calcite lattice. How that addition occurs is very poorly understood and is still a matter of debate. Surprisingly, when it occurs, although new atoms are introduced into the lattice, the result is shrinkage, which will fracture the

dolomitized rock, increasing its porosity! The dolomite rock is never made of pure dolomite minerals but is rather a mixture of calcite and dolomite. The mineral dolomite is slightly less soluble than calcite, yet there are significantly more caves known in limestones than in dolomites (for the same volume of rock). The reason for such a difference lies in the dolomite's tendency to crumble into fine dust (sometimes termed "dolomite flour") because of the jagged contour of the dolomite crystals (which first dissolve at the pointed tips, thus loosening the support between adjacent crystals). The calcite crystals in the limestone, on the other hand, have linear contours and they dissolve in depth without crumbling at a microscopic scale.

All karst features that occur in carbonate rocks mainly by dissolution are sometimes referred to as orthokarst (true karst).

Other types of sedimentary rocks also host many caves, some of them very large. Rock gypsum (calcium sulphate with two water molecules) is such a rock and also rock salt, both referred to as evaporite rocks (because they are believed to have been laid down by the evaporation of salty seawater). Evaporite rocks, however, are usually very pure, which suggests they were not deposited by evaporation after all (if they were exposed to the heat of the sun, they should be mixed with many different sediments) but rather by rapid deposition in the complex chemical underwater conditions generated by submarine volcanic activity.

Impurities 100%

Percentage of impurities

Mixed rocks with carbonate

e.g. calcareous sandstone dolomitic shale

50%   50%

Impure dolomite

(impure) Calcareous dolomite

(impure) Dolomitic limestone

Impure limestone

10%   10%

Dolomite

Calcareous dolomite

Dolomitic limestone

Limestone

Dolomite   90%   50%   10%   Calcite

End-member triangle for bulk classification of carbonate rocks

ROCK SALT

The evaporite karst, though not covering large surfaces, hosts some of the world's longest caves, all of them intricate labyrinths, sometimes over 124 miles (200 km) long.

Rock salt dissolves very easily in plain fresh water (without needing carbon dioxide like limestone). Most of the areas that have rock salt on the surface today are very arid and one would expect no significant caves to form in there. Yet it is exactly there that the world's longest caves in rock salt are located (Iran, Israel), which shows that these areas have been

The largest room in the Emil Racovitza Cave (a.k.a. Cinderella or Zolushka Cave) in the republic of Moldova. Most of the cave is an intricate labyrinth of intersecting narrow passages.

wet in the recent past (such caves do not need long time to form; in many recent salt mines, salt formations like stalactites and stalagmites have often grown to very large sizes). Such young ages are in accordance with the biblical timeframe.

Some smaller caves have also been found in chalk.

Unlike carbonate rocks, evaporite rocks are dissolved by dissociation:

$$NaCl + H_2O \leftrightarrows Na^{++} + Cl^-$$

Dissociation occurs faster than acid dissolution and this is why evaporite rocks are often intensely karsted (i.e., rich in karst features, especially caves). Karst in evaporites is referred to as parakarst ("near karst"). The term also applies to any karst-like form developed on other than carbonate rocks mainly by dissolution.

Caves and other karst-like features that formed in any rock other than by dissolution or dissociation processes are called pseudokarst ("false karst") and of them, the most spectacular are the ones in igneous rocks.

CAVES IN IGNEOUS ROCKS

One would not expect to find extensive caves in igneous rocks (rocks formed from molten materials) yet there are quite a few! There are either internal (endogenetic) or external (exogenetic) processes that can create caves in igneous rocks.

Endogenetic caves are formed within moving lava. Lava tubes are the most frequent and they can create vast networks of caves (the longest in the world, Kazumura Cave in Hawaii, is over 38 miles [61 km] long and spans over 3,200 feet [1,000 m] from the highest to the lowest point). Lava tubes form when and where there are long-term lava flows: the lava cools and solidifies at the surface but keeps flowing below. Once the flow stops and the lava drains out, a tube is left, roughly resembling a cave. Subsequent chemical and physical processes further shape the tubes, making them resemble limestone caves. Oftentimes, stalactites also form when abundant rainwater leaches minerals from the rock and redeposits them inside the caves.

Exogenetic caves are the result of either chemical processes (certain areas in the rock are chemically altered, becoming soft and subsequently washed away) or physical processes; as volcanic ash and other pyroclastics (rock fragments of all sorts and sizes, from ash to blocks, produced by volcanic blasts) are deposited, some voids are left — or, on rare occasions, big tree trunks and other organic material are buried and burned but their contour (mold) is preserved.

CAVES IN SEDIMENTARY ROCKS

a) Karstlands and their formation

Whichever way (dissociation or acid dissolution) the rock is removed, in order for the karsting processes to penetrate deep inside the rock, ways of access are needed. Karstic rocks usually offer them in the form of joints, cracks, faults, and bedding planes (the surfaces that separate layers). Many other rocks (even igneous ones) have extended networks of joints, cracks, and faults, but because they are much less soluble, the water simply accumulates inside those rocks until all the voids are filled. In limestone however, the accumulating water is believed to slowly eat away a part of the limestone, thus developing small conduits. Yet, unless that water were to move, proper caves would not form. What could cause this movement? Water cannot endlessly accumulate inside the rock; it has to exit somewhere. That exit point(s) has to be, obviously, lower than the input point(s). And finally, all the water-filled voids have to be interconnected so that once the water starts moving it does so from the top downward. The exit point(s) — called resurgences or karst springs — is in most cases located close to a river. In fact, it is believed that the river (the base level) is the one which, as it cuts into the rocks, eventually reaches the network of water-filled cracks, joints, and faults in the karst rocks, triggering the flow (drainage). Once the draining of the karst aquifer starts, the pace at which the enlargement of the karst conduits proceeds increases. Evolutionary karstologists believe that as the river deepens, the elevation of the resurgence follows it, lowering and creating a new, lower cave or lower passages of the existing caves. Thus, multi-level caves are believed to have formed. Evolutionary karstology claims that all of the processes that lead to the formation of mature caves and cave systems require tens or hundreds of thousands of years.

This subterranean drainage has a "partner" on the surface in the form of surface karst relief, which ensures the rapid transit of water from the surface to the underground. In a way, caves — the "underlandscape" — are a sort of negative image of the surface karst relief (landscape). This relief is very specific, unique

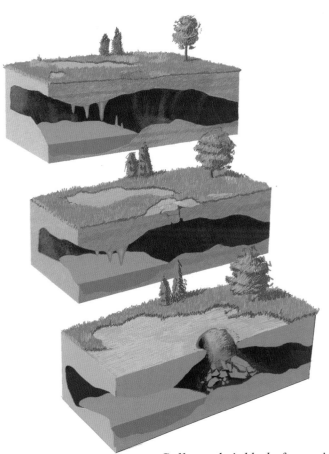

Collapsed sinkhole formation

33

in fact, and its archetype is found in the limestone terrains east of Trieste (Italy), in what is today Slovenia. Austrian geographers and geologists introduced the very name "karst" in the 19th century while they were studying the place. They actually Germanized the Slovenian name "Kras" used by the locals in that area. The word probably comes from an old pre-Indo-European root "kara" meaning "desert of stone." On a map from 1585 by the famous Dutch cartographer Mercator, the same area around Trieste is actually called "Karstia," which probably inspired the Germanization mentioned above. The Italians, on the other hand, call this type of landscape "carso."

While hiking in "Karstia," one would come across many unique forms of relief of all sizes. In many places where the limestone is barren, uncovered by soil, the rock is riddled with all sorts of runnels, grooves, and small hollows called karren (*lapiés* in France). When they cover large areas and the grooves intersect more or less at right angles, they are called limestone pavements (*lapiaz* in France). The acidic water that dissolved the limestone along joints and cracks forms these. Oftentimes, though, the karren form on smooth limestone surfaces, always following the slope, no matter how gentle. This shows that rainwater itself, without any soil to boost its CO_2 contents, can eat away a part of the limestone.

Funnel-shaped hollows, from a few feet to hundreds of feet in diameter, called sinkholes (dolines in Europe) often punctuate the terrain, like bomb craters. There are places in the world where their density is staggering, like the Lost River in Indiana where more than 360 sinkholes have been surveyed on 0.38 square miles (one square km)! When sinkholes merge (coalesce) a uvala usually forms, sometimes thousands of feet (hundreds of meters) in diameter.

The largest of all hollows (depressions) in karst terrains are called *polje* (yet another Slovenian word literally meaning "field"). Some measure over 62 miles (100 km) in length and 9.3 to 15.5 miles (15 to 25 km) in width, being surrounded by mountains and having a very flat bottom usually made of unbound sediment (gravel, sand, clay) which can be very thick. In the majority of cases, a river flows through the *polje*, usually emerging from a karst spring and sinking (returning underground) at the opposite end. Karstologists are far from being able to fully explain how poljes formed and this mysterious landform continues to intrigue scientists; many simply see poljes as huge windows opening over a river that flows underground.

Sometimes the rivers that flow on limestone terrains use very deep gorges with massive vertical walls, like huge caves with collapsed ceilings. In fact, in some cases there is clear evidence for that and sections of the ceiling are still preserved, looking like natural bridges.

Karst rivers, however, behave in unusual ways. When reaching the limestone terrains coming from other terrains (allochthonous valleys) they tend to sink into the rock. Some do that gradually through many points of infiltration until hardly any water is left on the surface. Others disappear suddenly through swallow holes or swallets (ponors in Europe) usually at the foot of a rock wall; these are called blind valleys. When they emerge at the surface, karst rivers are often

Sinkholes (dolines) in the Pădurea Craiului Mountains, Romania

natural bridge in Wayne County, Tennessee,
arved out by the sinkhole above

nature, with full strength and average flows
of up to 4,060.7 cubic feet per second (115
m³/s) (115 tons of water every second, enough
to supply the needs of more than two New
York cities every day!). These karst springs
are called emergences (when there is no evidence of the origin of the waters that emerge)
or resurgences (the re-emergence of a known
stream). Larger springs are often located at
the foot of an escarpment in a sort of reversed
blind valley called a pocket valley. One of the
largest and most beautiful is the one at Vaucluse in southern France where the very archetype of a karst spring — Fontaine de Vaucluse
— lies. This vallis clausa (Latin for "closed
valley") starts at the foot of a 984 foot-high (300 m)
limestone wall and it discharges an average of 1,024
cubic feet (29 cubic meters) per second. But what is
really impressive about this emergence is its 984.25-
feet-plus (300 m) deep flooded shaft whose bottom
was reached only by a remotely operated vehicle.

*The most famous karst spring in
the world — Fontaine de Vaucluse — near Avignon, southern
France, is the source of the river
Sorgue.*

The periodic and
rhythmic springs are
probably the most in-
teresting of them all,
being only found in
karstlands. Fontaine
de Fontestorbes in
southern France is the
most complete and
spectacular example
on record. From July
until October (and in
very dry years until
January) this spring
becomes intermit-
tent. It flows (with an
average discharge of
423 gallons or 1,600
liters per second) for
36 minutes and 36
seconds, then in a
few minutes comes to
a halt (just a trickle of
water is left) which
lasts 32 minutes and
30 seconds. The full
flow is then restored
within few minutes
and the whole mecha-
nism functions with
a precision to the
second. This unusual
behavior is due to the
very special shape
and spatial distribu-
tion of the caves and conduits involved, as well as the
constancy of water supply to the caves.

Many of the surface and even subterranean karst
forms can be found on rocks other than karstic rocks
(in quartzites, granites, and other igneous rocks).

High flow

Low flow

Fontaine de Fontestorbes

Fontaine de Fontestorbes in southern France

They are usually called pseudokarst ("false karst"), though incorrectly. The karsting process is the result of chemical erosion (as opposed to mechanical erosion) of a substrate. Only when the forms are not the result of chemical erosion, regardless of the substrate, is the term "pseudokarst" appropriate. As mentioned earlier, the term "parakarst" is more appropriate in such cases.

b) Non-karstic terrains

One of the most surprising areas to have revealed parakarst features is the quartzite sandstones (sandstone formed predominantly of quartz and which has silica as cement) in Northeastern South America (Venezuela and British Guiana). Huge caves have been found there, with massive rivers flowing through

them. Quartz and silica, however, are not really soluble in carbon dioxide-rich water, so a standard karsting process is very difficult to imagine even over extended periods of time. In fact, until these caves were discovered in recent years, it was believed that extensive parakarstic features on quartzite were impossible. However, some other unusual karst terrains like the Guadalupe Mountains in New Mexico (where the famous Carlsbad Caverns are) have suggested a possible explanation for the quartzite parakarst. Many scientists agree today that the Carlsbad Caverns and the rest of the karst in the area are the result of the limestone being dissolved by sulfuric acid rising (not seeping down as in the case of proper karsting) from hydrocarbon reservoirs in the adjacent Ramsey Sands. In Lechuguilla Cave (linked to Carlsbad) vast amounts of gypsum bear witness to the reaction of sulfuric acid with limestone:

$$CaCO_3 + H_2SO_4 + 2H_2O \rightarrow CaSO_4 \cdot 2H_2O \text{ (gypsum)} + CO_2$$

Sulfuric acid eats away limestone much faster than carbonic acid does. Calculations have shown, for example, that the Big Room in Carlsbad Caverns, one of the world's largest cave chambers (over 35 million cubic feet or one million cubic meters) could have been excavated by the amount of sulfuric acid produced in the adjacent sands during one year. This discovery has drastically changed even the signs posted at the caves. From 1924 to 1988, there was a visitor's sign above the entrance to Carlsbad Caverns that said Carlsbad was at least 260 million years old. In 1988, the sign was changed to read 7 to 10 million years old. Then, for a little while, the sign read that it was 2 million years old. Now the sign is gone. (Jerry Trout [cave specialist with the National Forest Service], "Descent," *Arizona Highways*, Jan. 1993, p. 10–11.)

It is therefore quite possible that quartzite caves, too, have been excavated by acids other than carbonic, in very different geological conditions and very quickly.

CARLSBAD CAVERNS
NEW MEXICO

CHAPTER FOUR

CLASSIFYING CAVES

There are two basic types of caves: 1) active (live) (i.e., caves which have a flowing stream in them, fossil) and 2) relict (i.e., caves without a flowing stream in them [but which may still have ponds and dripping water]).

Active caves can be of three main types:

a1. inflow caves–caves into which a stream sinks and which are only partly accessible to humans.

a2. outflow caves–caves from which a stream emerges and which are partly accessible to humans.

a3. through caves–caves traversed by a stream and traversable to humans, too.

In inflow and outflow caves, human penetration is hindered or even prevented when the water completely floods the cave passage, forming sumps.

According to their position in regard to the water table, caves can be: vadose caves (active, above the water table), water table caves, phreatic caves (below

the water table), or compoundrelict (fossil caves above the water table).

If a cave opens to the surface through a shaft (pit) and continues with more pits connected by more or less horizontal passages, it is referred to as a pothole. Some of the subterranean shafts (pits) are huge, dwarfing anyone descending into them. The famous bell-shaped Sótano de las Golondrinas in Mexico has a sheer vertical drop of 1,233 feet (376 m) with a diameter at the base of 180 feet (55 m). It is one of the most popular sites in the world for base jumping (parachuting without a plane).

Some caves are linear, with a main passage extending mostly in one direction. Others branch out into intricate mazes. The world's second longest cave, Optimisticeskaya (in Ukraine) unfolds its 132.9 miles (214 km) of passageways within an area of roughly 0.38 square miles (1 km²)!

Most caves develop along one main level but some develop on several vertical levels with quite intricate three-dimensional mazes.

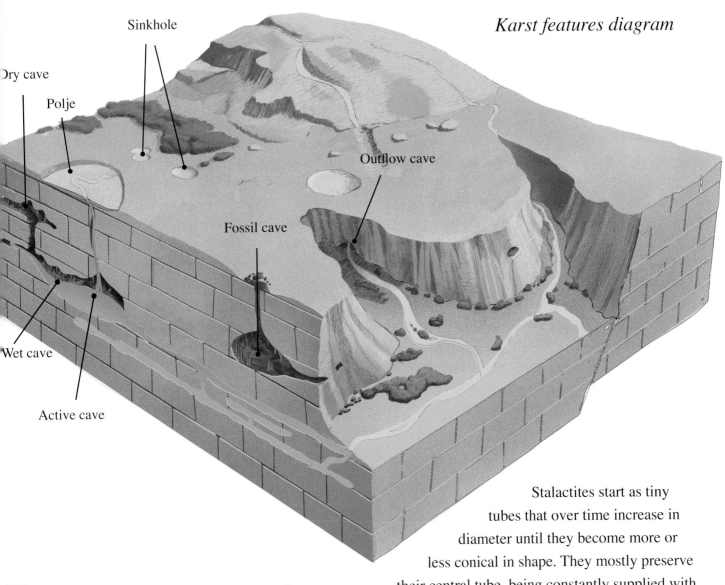

Dry cave

Sinkhole

Polje

Outflow cave

Fossil cave

Wet cave

Active cave

THE STUFF IN CAVES

Several different types of items can be found in caves:

Secondary crystalline formations (speleothems).

These are the spectacular "cave decorations" that make caves such popular tourist attractions. They are "secondary" because they formed after the caves-proper formed, as a result of infiltrating, calcite-charged waters, or of various local mineralizing solutions. They can be:

Dripping speleothems: stalactites (hanging from the ceiling), stalagmites (growing from the floor), and columns (when a stalactite and a stalagmite merge).

Stalactites start as tiny tubes that over time increase in diameter until they become more or less conical in shape. They mostly preserve their central tube, being constantly supplied with drip water. In a few cases, the original tube retains its diameter and a soda straw (tubular stalactite) will start growing. This tiny, translucent calcite tube can exceptionally reach several feet in length! In most cases, though, such tubes break under their own weight. Stalagmites are deposited one layer on top of the other, usually thicker at the base and narrowing toward the tip. Their shape and size varies enormously, some reaching tens of feet in height.

Gravitational flow speleothems: flowstone, draperies, rimstone.

Once water reaches a cave, gravity makes it flow toward the water table. On its way there, it will give up most of its mineral load, generating a variety of speleothems. Flowstone forms wherever water flows in thin films (laminar flow) over a larger area, usually starting on a wall and continuing on the floor.

Draperies form on the ceilings and walls as thin sheets with the appearance of curtains, sometimes smooth, sometimes wavy. When thin, translucent, and with colored bands in them, some people call them "bacon" because of the striking resemblance to that popular food item.

Rimstone precipitates on the rim of overflowing pools, initially as a thin blade that in time may grow into a solid dam up to 12 feet high. Rimstone pools form behind such dams.

Capillary flow speleothems: shields, cave coral (popcorn), eccentrics.

When water flows through very narrow (less than one millimeter wide) conduits, it can sometimes defy gravity and flow upward! The mineral load it carries can be deposited (precipitated) into all sorts of surprising speleothems. Shields are in a way a very special type of drapery. Two semicircular plates start growing parallel to each other on the left and right sides of a narrow (capillary) crack. They can grow in any direction but the most striking are the ones that grow steeply upward. Shields can reach more than three feet in diameter and eventually water starts flowing over their edge, the plate (tabular) growth becoming a normal flowstone growth, so that the shield often looks like a fringed canopy.

Cave coral (popcorn in North America) are

Dog tooth spar

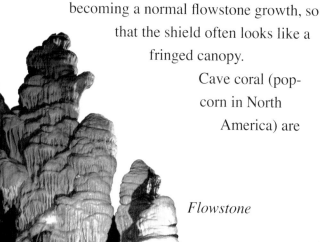

Flowstone

essentially globular individual or clustered speleothems that may resemble coral or grapes.

Their origin is not well understood and there are several theories regarding their formation. It is most probable, though, that capillary flow is involved. Eccentrics are by far the most spectacular and admired speleothems. They are made of very pure calcite crystals growing "eccentrically," (i.e., in any spatial direction), often against gravity. When growing from stalactites (or ceiling and wall) they are called helictites; when growing from stalagmites (and floor) they are called heligmites. Though capillary flow is again most probably involved, exactly how remains a mystery to this day. My personal research has suggested that natural electrical charges may also be involved.

Pool speleothems: spars, shelfstone, cave (calcite) rafts, cave pearls.

Oftentimes, the water that infiltrates caves accumulates in pools. Whenever that water is saturated in calcite, wonderful things start happening. The walls become covered with large dogtooth spar calcite crystals. If there are any stalactites reaching into the pools, their submerged parts will be covered with the same spar. The same happens with the submerged parts of stalagmites. Sometimes the rims of the pools are lined with shelfstone, horizontal ledges of calcite always marking the surface of the water. When pool water is saturated and also very calm (no water dripping into it from above), thin flakes of calcite start growing, floating on the water — hence their name, cave rafts. When they become too heavy, they sink to the bottom of the ponds where they can accumulate in quite thick layers.

The most spectacular of pool speleothems are cave pearls. They usually grow in shallow pools, layer after layer of smooth calcite or aragonite over all sorts of fragments like sand grains, chips of limestone, etc. Some of them are nearly spherical, some more or less irregular, and there are even polygonal ones (with angular facets). Their formation is only partially understood, especially the reason for their sphericity, since they lie on the bottom of ponds and should have a flat bottom. Various scenarios of periodic rolling have been suggested, but none accounts for all recorded features.

NON-CALCITE SPELEOTHEMS

Speleothems can also be classified by their mineral composition. Although the vast majority of speleothems are made of calcite (trigonal $CaCO_3$) and aragonite (rhombic $CaCO_3$), several thousand other minerals have been found in caves. The most frequent are sulfates of which gypsum is the real star, taking many different forms, from gypsum flowers (anthodites) to balloons and various types of crusts. In Lechuguilla Cave (New Mexico) there are huge pendants called "chandeliers" made of pure white gypsum, nearly 33 feet (up to 10 meters) long! A very rare sulfate mineral that usually appears as fine needles (angel hair) is mirabilite ($Na_2SO_4 \cdot 10H_2O$). One location in which

Carlsbad Caverns, New Mexico. Cave pearls. These pearls are caused by layers of rock building up over a grain of sand, just like pearls in an oyster.

mirabilite behaves very unusually is the cave Izvorul Tăuşoarelor in northern Romania.

The mineral there appeared sometime between 1972 and 1974 and rapidly grew, covering a part of the floor in a room situated 640 feet (200 m) below the surface. Within four years, it even "hopped" a few hundred meters away, starting to grow on the floor of a small aired passage. A few years later, it started waning to near extinction at the end of a two-year period only to wax again afterward. The waxing and waning behavior continues to this day. My research has indicated that besides electrical charges, airborne particles are also involved in the formation of these special speleothems. Recent research by others seems to confirm that.

Close-up of mirabilite (angel hair)

Moonmilk (believed in the Middle Ages to form in caves because of the moon's rays) is a cheese-like soft agglomerate of various carbonate microcrystals. It usually mimics various other speleothems and sometimes, when plastic enough, it can even slowly flow over escarpments as a white, viscous waterfall. Besides its alchemic uses in the Middle Ages, moonmilk is traditionally used in some European countries to successfully treat cattle mastitis.

Ice forms in most caves of temperate and cold climates, usually in the entrance areas as ice stalagmites and stalactites. Sometimes ice stalagmites are shaped like a series of sphere-like bulbs, one on top of another and connected by cylindrical segments. The ice in the bulbs is clear, sometimes almost transparent, while in the cylindrical sections the ice is milky white and opaque. The spherical sections represent periods of time when the air temperature was around 24.8°F (-4° C) — the ideal crystallizing temperature for ice — so that as it slowly formed, ice expelled the air in the water. The opaque sections formed when the temperature was significantly lower, freezing was rapid, and lots of air bubbles became trapped in the ice. Such ice stalagmites can therefore be used as temperature markers.

In some caves, ice is known to have accumulated as perennial blocks at the bottom of shafts and cave chambers, like miniature captive glaciers. The world's largest (volume-wise) subterranean glacier is in the Dobsinska Cave in Slovakia (approximately 3.8 million cubic feet or 110 thousand cubic meters of ice), followed by Romania's Scărişoara Cave (approximately

Seasonal ice forming at the mouth of a cave on Grand Island, Lake Superior, Michigan's Upper Peninsula, USA

2.6 million cubic feet or 75,000 cubic meters) and Austria's Eisriesenwelt (approximately 1.7 million cubic feet or 50,000 cubic meters).

The first two are cold air traps (i.e., deep caves opening to the surface through vertical shafts). Cold air falls into the shafts and the cul-de-sac rooms beyond, cooling the rock walls. The warm air during the summer cannot displace the heavier cold air at the bottom, and the following winter more cold air will accumulate in the lower sections. Thus, the temperature in these cold air traps remains below the freezing point until late spring or early summer. All the water infiltrating from the surface will therefore freeze inside. If enough water infiltrates, ice blocks start building, acting like the cooling elements in an ice box, thus making the entire cave more resistant to warming. The temperature inside these ice blocks never reaches melting point so that they are preserved over many years.

Eisriesenwelt, on the other hand, is a dynamic cave, and it has lower and upper entrances located at high elevations (the lower entrance is above 5,248 feet [1,600 m] in the Austrian Alps). In wintertime, cold air is sucked through the lower entrance as warm air exits through the upper ones. Consequently, the rock walls are cooled below the freezing point (just like in the previous case) and when the first spring meltwater infiltrates into the lower section of the cave, it freezes, creating an ice block. Because the lower entrance narrows significantly within the first 150 feet (50 m), the volume of cold air flowing out through it in the summer (when the circuit reverses — see the cave climate section) is not enough to allow sufficient warmer air to completely melt the ice and thus the ice is preserved inside the cave.

Detrital formations

These are, in essence, sediments brought into the caves by the streams that traverse them and residual material left by the limestone dissolved by such streams and infiltrating water. Gravel, sand, and clay are the main

HUMAN ARTIFACTS

Some of the most significant human artifacts have actually been found in caves, from tools to sanctuaries and burial sites. Human habitation, like the one in the famous cave Zhoukoudian in China (where the renowned Peking Man was discovered), seems to have unfolded over extensive periods of time, leaving behind, among other things, thick layers of ash from the continuous fires the inhabitants kept alive.

Archaeological excavation of a site at the Lazaret caves in southern France (right). These caves have yielded a wide range of early human remains and artifacts.

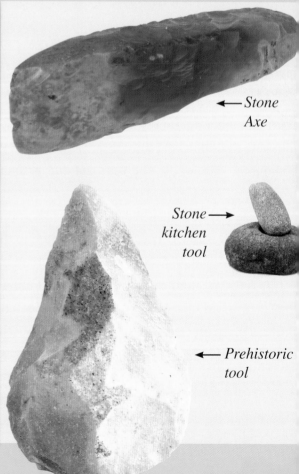

← *Stone Axe*

Stone → *kitchen tool*

← *Prehistoric tool*

constituents of these sediments and they can sometimes be found very high above the streams, on ledges, or sometimes completely filling large cave passages — silent witnesses of turbulent flooding episodes that scoured the caves.

ORGANIC MATERIAL

This consists of various vegetal debris washed into caves, as well as the remains of various animals that lived and died in caves or were washed into them. Human remains in caves are always of extreme importance because they represent — in the vast majority of cases — people of a distant past.

THE DATING OF SPELEOTHEMS

Speleothems are nearly pure calcite that was removed from the limestone and redeposited inside caves. When removed (by carbonic acid) from the limestone, some other soluble minerals accompany calcite, and some contain the radioisotope uranium 234 (^{234}U). This decays through a long series of intermediates into lead 206 (^{206}Pb). One important intermediate is another radioisotope, thorium 230 (^{230}Th), which is insoluble. When a stalagmite starts forming, inside the calcite some ^{234}U atoms will also be present. If ^{230}Th is also found, it is assumed it only came from the ^{234}U in the stalagmite. If then:

1) the initial number of ^{234}U atoms in the stalagmite is known;
2) the rate of decay is known;
3) there was no ^{230}Th alongside ^{234}U in the beginning;
4) and neither of the two radioisotopes was added or leached out from the stalagmite after it started forming, then the age of that stalagmite can be calculated.

It is quite obvious that there are too many unknowns or uncontrollable parameters in this series of assumptions to make radiometric dating of speleothems accurate. Regardless of these problems, evolutionary scientists consider it one of the most accurate radiometric dating methods! Many thousands of such datings have been performed, with some speleothems claimed to have been growing over periods longer than 100,000 years. This means that the dripping point (the place where the speleothem-building water reaches a cave) could not have changed during all that time. And this is assumed to be valid not only for the dated speleothems but for all of them, millions upon millions worldwide! Such constancy, though, runs counter to the field data. The intricate path infiltrating water follows from the surface to the dripping point is represented mainly by very small conduits (joints, cracks, bedding planes). The water flowing along them is supposed to constantly dissolve the walls of the conduit, therefore enlarging it. This means the parameters of the flow will constantly change and that is known to happen in a timeframe much shorter than the tens and hundreds of thousands of years assigned to many speleothems.

The measured rate at which limestone is removed by dissolution at the surface of the terrain (denudation rate) is well over 1 cm every thousand years on the average. This, however, is removal on a surface, but inside the limestone the removal is through the entire rock pile so that the speleothem-feeding conduits enlarge significantly in short periods of time.

The pace of precipitation (and consequently the pace at which a crystalline structure is built) of soluble minerals (including the ones precipitating as speleothems) varies from mineral to mineral. Some minerals like hydromganesite do precipitate faster than calcite but the difference is irrelevant for the alleged "measured" long ages of speleothems. Calcite speleothems have definitely been recorded growing very quickly. The regular-size stalagmite in this picture grew out of an abandoned can. Although not pure calcite, the speed at which this stalagmite grows is still a visual challenge to the idea that speleothems need a very long time to grow.

This would alter the flow of water and the position of the dripping point. It is therefore very difficult to accept the idea that dripping point positions are stable during tens and hundreds of millennia! To add to this problem, changes on the surface like growth/extinction of forests, permafrost (during the Ice Age), etc. will also significantly affect the dripping points. There are many recorded instances in which cutting the forest above a cave led to the drying out and "death" of speleothems.

In addition to all these, there are recorded cases in which speleothems grew very quickly. I have seen lab dishes we used in caves to collect dripwater covered by a thick (up to 1 cm) calcite crust in less than ten years. In the Cripple Creek Gold Mine in Colorado, stalagmites and stalactites over a meter long have grown in less than 100 years!

Let us go back to a "standard" case inferred in the scientific literature: if a 3.2 ft. (one-meter) stalagmite were dated to 100,000 years of growth, its annual growth rate must have averaged 0.00039 in. (0.01 mm) per year. This is ten times slower than the slowest measured today! Evolutionary scientists try to explain this by saying that the growth occasionally stopped completely, perhaps for 10,000 years at a time, after that, resuming at the regular growth rate of say 0.0039 in. (0.1 mm) per year. In other words, they assume that after 10,000 years, nothing changed. The dripping point was not affected at all, the water drops arriving again at exactly the same point, with millimeter precision! Some experienced karstologists would find that quite difficult to accept, though.

All of the above mean that direct measurements and logic indicate that the assumptions on which the radiometric dating of speleothems is built are seriously flawed and consequently the dates yielded are highly questionable.

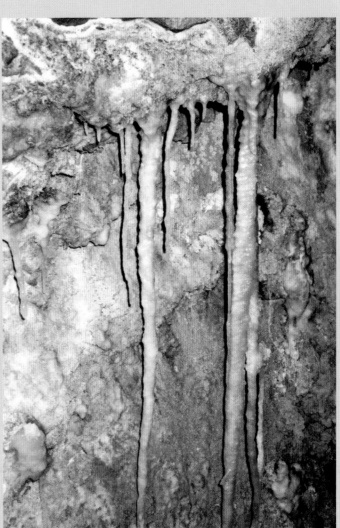

This classical set of speleothems — stalactites, stalagmites, columns, and even soda straws — formed in less than a century. The colorations are due to various metallic components like copper and iron, yet most of the crystalline material is calcite. Soda straws are good evidence for that since the only non-calcite soda straws recorded are the salt ones.

CHAPTER FIVE

EXPLORING CAVES

Caves are a unique environment in which darkness, humidity, and many physical obstacles represent a serious challenge. Besides needing to be in good physical condition, cave explorers need proper equipment. They have to fight not only colder temperatures, but also humidity; body heat is lost very quickly in caves because of it. Therefore insulation is a major factor in the clothing used in caves.

The coverall is the most popular piece of clothing among cavers, not only because of durability but also because, unlike any other type of clothing, it does not roll up or down in the tightest crawls, turning the caver into a cork! There are waterproof coveralls as well as normal fabric ones. The former are essential in wet caves; the latter are more suitable in drier caves. Breathable waterproof fabrics are still too expensive to be commonly used in this very harsh and abrasive environment.

In the past, cumbersome inflatable boats explored

river caves. Nowadays, wetsuits worn under a coveralls are the way to go, swimming and walking through the water — much faster and involving less effort.

Lighting is essential in caves and there are two basic types in use: open flame from burning acetylene (coming from calcium carbide and water in a generator hanging on the side of the caver) and electric. The open flame provides a much richer light and covers larger surfaces but is considered cumbersome, especially by North American cavers, who prefer electric lights. However, because of the very high humidity, the light beam from an electric bulb is not spread enough and vision is limited to a rather narrow circle. With the advent of LED flashlights, the dispersion of light has improved, but still, the best light comes from an open flame. The best is, in fact, a combination of the two, a dual headlight, with the burner of acetylene mounted on the top of an LED flashlight.

This will allow the caver to have his light on even when the flame is extinguished by water while descending or traversing a waterfall. Whichever the type, the light source is located on the helmet that cavers wear.

As for footwear, some prefer hiking boots, some prefer rubber boots. Gloves are also part of the personal equipment because the limestone and especially clays inside caves dry human skin very quickly.

Whenever cave exploration requires tackling vertical drops, the single rope technique (SRT) is used which means that both descending (abseiling or rappelling) and ascending are done by way of special tools attached to a rope and the caver. Various techniques are available using descenders (braking devices) and ascenders and a harness that attaches the devices to the caver.

The ultimate frontier to explore in caves is underwater. Many caves have flooded passages; some caves are completely flooded. Exploring these caves is one of the most dangerous human enterprises and one of the main sources of cave casualties. When diving in a cave, there are three main danger factors unique to this environment:

a) The fact that in case of an emergency, the explorer cannot simply ascend to the surface, he/she needs to retrace all the way back. This is why the iron rule is the "one-third rule": one only advances into a flooded cave till a third of the air supply is used up. The second third is left for the return while the third is kept in case of any emergency.

b) The very reduced ability humans have to find their bearings underwater. This is why a guideline

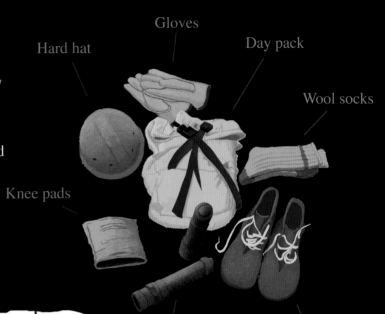

Hard hat

Gloves

Day pack

Wool socks

Knee pads

Flashlights

Boots

CAVE DIVING

Standard diving equipment, circa 1878.

Alexander the Great, in 325 B.C., was apparently the first to build and use a diving device (a sort of barrel with an opening that could trap an air bubble inside) to study submarine life. In 1680, the Italian physicist Borelli built and used the first proper diving equipment, a leather pouch filled with air, connected to the diver's mouth. He also invented a sort of socks with fins for better propulsion. The first recorded cave dive was Cavolini's visit of the submarine caves in the Bay of Naples, in 1785, using a diving bell. In 1878, Ottonelli descended 75 feet (23 meters) inside Fontaine de Vaucluse using the heavy diving equipment (Siebe – Gorman), with a large metallic helmet, rubber suit, heavy boots, and air lines connected to the surface. Using the same equipment, dive attempts were made in caves in Switzerland (1893, 1934) and Austria (1894). Soon after co-inventing the Aqualung, Jaques-Yves Cousteau was the first to SCUBA dive inside a cave (1946), and his choice was Fontaine de Vaucluse! He and his companion reached 151 feet (46 m) and nearly died because of carbon monoxide intoxication.

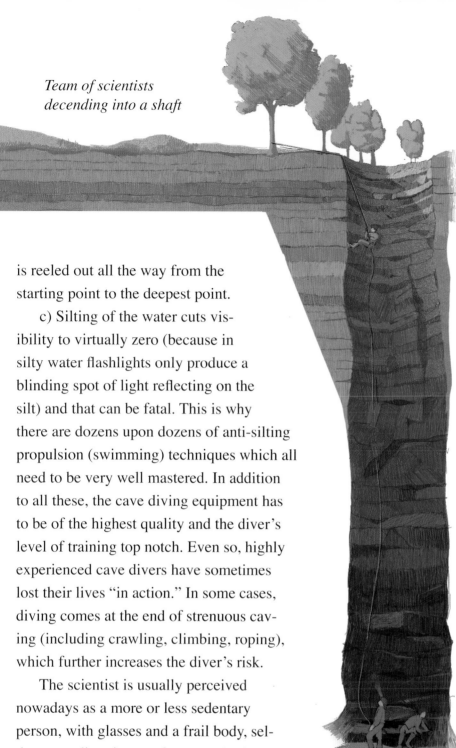

Team of scientists decending into a shaft

ALL IN A DAY'S WORK

Let us follow a team of scientists for a long and tiring research day trip to a complex cave. As we travel with them, we can learn not only some of the basics of cave exploration but also how their science is applied to help them reach as far as possible into the belly of the earth. And while doing this, we will discover some new karst features and learn some more of the scientific language these modern cavemen use.

After attaching the rope to a big tree (the ideal anchoring for all cavers) and ensuring the rope is not damaged by sharp rocks, the team of three begins the descent down the rope, carefully stepping over the edge after clearing loose rocks. Once the rim is passed, with the tips of their boots rhythmically touching the wall, they swing down the rope one by one, looking for the best holds and the safest trajectory that avoids loose rocks and sharp edges. As they descend, the smell of life (leaves, flowers, trees) gradually gives way to the smell of death — the rotting plant debris that has fallen into the shaft, some of it resting on the many ledges in the walls, most at the bottom of the shaft, which is now visible.

Landing in a black muck composed mostly of rotten leaves and wood, they can hear the sound of flowing water farther below. Far above "hangs" the narrow, nearly round mouth of the shaft, a bright white with the dark blue sky beyond. Below, behind a huge, half-rotten log, there is a narrow opening through which

is reeled out all the way from the starting point to the deepest point.

c) Silting of the water cuts visibility to virtually zero (because in silty water flashlights only produce a blinding spot of light reflecting on the silt) and that can be fatal. This is why there are dozens upon dozens of anti-silting propulsion (swimming) techniques which all need to be very well mastered. In addition to all these, the cave diving equipment has to be of the highest quality and the diver's level of training top notch. Even so, highly experienced cave divers have sometimes lost their lives "in action." In some cases, diving comes at the end of strenuous caving (including crawling, climbing, roping), which further increases the diver's risk.

The scientist is usually perceived nowadays as a more or less sedentary person, with glasses and a frail body, seldom spending time on fitness and other physical activities. The cave scientist, however, has to deploy a significant amount of effort, and also needs to master various climbing and diving techniques, all while keeping a clear mind and the ability to focus on very specific scientific issues. Oftentimes he/she has to return to the surface with a good load of rock samples, which adds to the effort. These are all good reasons why there are so few cave scientists to this day.

hey crawl on their bellies into a pipe-like, winding passage which descends to a small opening. Beyond it a wide space opens, a huge shaft coming from far above and plunging into the darkness. About 32 feet (10 m) below their feet the waters of a powerful stream seem to explode into the shaft from a side passage, the misty spray reflecting light like a white screen.

After attaching the rope to two spits they plant into the wall, they descend past the waterfall, carefully avoiding the copious amounts of water hurtling down the shaft. At the bottom of the shaft, 114 feet (35 m) below the opening, the water recollects into a stream that rushes down a narrow and very high passage, which they follow.

Within a few twists and turns, near-silence replaces the rumbling and hissing of the waterfall. The smooth-ly flowing stream makes very little noise, much less than the friction of their gear against the walls. This silence is not at all promising, as it usually signals the most disliked obstacle: a sump. In a few minutes, the high ceiling suddenly starts plummeting and it soon reaches the still surface of a pond. It is a sump, and for a moment they feel disappointed; so much effort, only to have the cave end so abruptly.

temperature (44.96°F or 7.2°C) is nearly one degree colder than any of the karst springs and that means this water still has to travel a lot inside the rock to gain that extra degree in temperature. That is good news! There might be other passages shortcutting the sump and if they are there, the air should move through them. There are many passages above the stream and one of them has a significant air draft: the way forward! The air moves upstream and that is important informa-tion: it means there are significant voids beyond the sump but there has to be another sump that cannot be shortcut. It is mid-summer and the colder air from the upper sections of the cave flows toward the lower exit, so if there were a continuous aired connection be-tween the two entrances, the air in this passage should flow downstream. In order to move in the opposite direction, the cold air brought by the waterfall (which acts like a pump) needs to reach larger chambers or a lengthy system of passages in which it warms and starts ascending through alternative passages.

They begin a long crawl along a narrow, winding, pipe-like passage. Soon the one passage becomes a

The team crawls through narrow passages.

But this cannot be the final sump, the place where the stream disappears only to reappear into daylight through a spring (resurgence). There are several of those above the ground and they know one of them has to carry the water from this cave. This stream's

maze, almost like a honeycomb with tubular passages intersecting at angles ranging from 45 to 60 degrees.

This is because the passages follow joints and faults (master joints). The smooth surface of the walls is interrupted every now and then by spoon-shaped

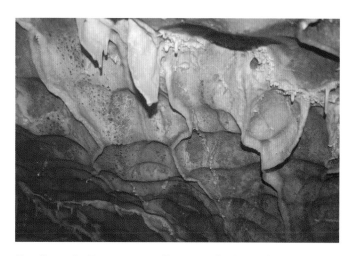

Scallops in Resonance Cave, B.C. Canada.

scoops called scallops. They are asymmetric, with the steepest slope always pointing upstream. Many ceiling (dissolution) pockets (dome-shaped or chimney-shaped cavities in the ceiling of the passages) are also present, confirming that these passages formed under or in the near vicinity of the water table, an environment known as phreatic, or saturated. The water, most probably in the presence of excess carbon dioxide (possibly from accumulating rotting organic matter) has dissolved the rock in the ceiling and kept rising until it reached the water table level.

After more than 30 minutes spent on their elbows and knees and many times on their bellies, the team reaches an area where narrow pits lurk in the floor with funnel-shaped mouths covered by slippery mud and clay brought up there by the swollen stream during floods. Sometimes the pressure of the water below is so high that when it bursts into the upper levels it can carry large boulders with it! Soon the familiar sound of flowing water can clearly be heard coming from a pit large enough to allow their bodies to slide down the rope, like corks pushed downward into a bottleneck. The stream below flows in a low, large passage with an elliptical section and a perfectly level ceiling. Downstream, the shape of the passage changes, with layers of sediments (sand and gravel) sloping from the side walls toward the stream. The top of the sediments is covered by a fine

layer of dusty clay often cracked in polygonal shapes as it dried (desiccation cracks), a sign that there haven't been any floods in the recent past (a long time is needed in order for a clay like this to dry in an atmosphere with a humidity over 90 percent). Thin, tubular soda straws hang above by the dozens, continuously dripping on top of the sediments, resulting in a thin layer of flowstone gradually covering the clay.

To the great and pleasant surprise of the scientists, on the left bank resting on its side lays the complete, undisturbed skeleton of a cave bear! This is a real treat, as the vast majority of such skeletons — and there are probably hundreds of thousands of them in many caves in the Northern Hemisphere where the animal once lived — are jumbled up. In fact, there are less than five such complete, undisturbed skeletons known in the entire world! The skull is already covered with a thin film of calcite — a simple and elegant burial feature. By the size of the skull and the teeth, this must have been an old adult that entered the cave to die (or maybe to hibernate), obviously following a different path from that of the scientists. This is good evidence that the cave looked different at the time of the Ice Age when these creatures chose to use caves as a long-term residence, only exiting for feeding.

Cave bears were troglophiles and spent most of their life in caves, where they mated and females delivered their young. Many gestation holes have been found, dug by pregnant females in soft clay, in which they not only lay more comfortably but also could shelter their offspring better.

Looking for a possible ancient access for this bear, they notice a pile of rubble that marks the presence of a side chamber opening in the left wall of the passage. A wide, sloping passage leads to the chamber, which is unfortunately terminated by a huge mass of breakdown blocks coming from the walls and ceiling. Beyond it is undoubtedly the access the bear used to reach his resting place. The changes on the mountain slope where the old entrance probably was have caused the collapse of the

RECORD	Name	Location	Cumulated length of passages in kilometers (miles)	Depth (from top to bottom)	Dimentions
Longest cave	Mammoth cave – Flint Ridge	Kentucky, USA	579 (359.774)		
Longest underwater cave	Ox Bel Ha	Yucatán Peninsula, Mexico	134 (83.264)		
Longest cave in rock gypsum	Optimistices—Kaya Cave	Ukraine	214 (132.973)		
Longest cave in rock salt	Cave in the Queshm Geopark	Iran	Over 6 (3.728)		
Deepest cave	Voronya Cave	Republic of Georgia		2,140 meters (7,020 ft. 11 in.)	
Deepest cave dive (by ROV)	Fontaine de Vaucluse	France		315 meters (1,033 ft. 5 in.)	
Deepest cave dive (by humans)	Bushmansgat Cave	South Africa		282.6 meters (927 ft. 1 in.)	
Deepest underwater karst shaft	El Zacatón	Mexico		At least 329 meters (at least 1,079 ft.)	
Largest underground chamber	Sarawak Chamber	Gunung Mulu National Park, Borneo, Malaysia			600 x 400 x 80 meters 1,968 x 1,312 x 262 ft.
Deepest cave shaft	Vrtoglavica Cave	Slovenia		603 meters (1,978 ft. 4 in.)	
Longest time spent in cave	Popowa Yama Cave	Ukraine	The Stermers, a Jewish family from Ukraine, spent nearly two years hiding in the cave from Nazis and their collaborators.		

feet (50 m) away. However, the light ends in darkness to the right, ahead, and behind. This can only mean one thing: they are in the middle of a huge chamber. Days later, after the painstaking survey is finished, a huge chamber is revealed: 2,013 feet (615 m) long, 511 feet (156 m) wide, and over 147 feet (45 m) high! That is about half the size of the largest known cave chamber in Sarawak, Borneo. The sheer size of this chamber requires a larger exploration team and at least one full day to investigate, but they are already tired and the work day is far from being finished. Now they will start the survey and take it as close as they can to the entrance, before

entrance and it's clogged with debris. The lack of roots and wooden material in the breakdown pile is an indication that the surface is still far away. Once the cave survey is finished, they will be able to trace this passage on the surface looking for signs of the old entrance.

Back in the main passage, the team continues downstream to a waterfall and past it they reach a series of huge blocks among which the water soon disappears. They carefully climb toward the highest point in order to find their bearings in this huge chaos of blocks. Once on top, a powerful electric torch is switched on and the bluish-white beacon of light slices through a vast void. The ceiling is clearly visible some 100 feet (30 m) above. To the left, the wall is also visible about 170

their tired bodies and minds give the signal all experienced cavers would know: time to get out! One wrong bearing and the whole day's work will be lost!

The survey is just the first step in the meticulous work of recording all the needed data. After that they will record the scientific data concerning geology, geomorphology, karstology, sedimentology, and paleontology. The cave bear remains will need many hours of careful work. And when all that is finished, several days later, they'll have to return for photography. And that will not be all since there are many more passages left unexplored. Many more visits are needed until this cave will have revealed all its secrets. Quite possibly some of those secrets will trigger more surface research, which might even lead to the discovery of new caves.

All of these things are good news for scientists whose second habitat is caves. Yes, they love the adrenaline rush which comes with the ability to walk into places untouched by any human foot since the beginning of time — and that in their own country, not in some remote and expensive-to-reach corner of the planet. Being down there in the absolute darkness, with dramatic and noisy passages alternating with places of absolute stillness and perfect silence, is part of a unique experience that takes a human being much closer to God.

I remember so vividly how I used to sometimes lie on my back in soft sand, waiting for my companions to return after we had spread out individually exploring different passages. I would turn my lights off and listen to "the sound of silence." Absolute silence is an impossible situation for our brain which, when deprived of any audio stimulation, creates imaginary sounds just to stay busy! So I would hear all sorts of strange things, from the real sounds of my body to voices of the past, even choirs. And with my eyes wide open, I would stare into the absolute darkness, sometimes seeing light. Later, after my dear wife, Flory, brought me to the Lord, I would spend time with Him in the darkness and see the light of God! What better place to see the Light than in the belly of the earth?!

I often learned useful lessons down there. I remember falling asleep and not hearing my companions coming back. As they got close to me I would suddenly awake and their lights would painfully blind my eyes. I needed five minutes to completely regain my sight and the pain was very real. Later I thought about Christians entering the homes of people who didn't know Christ, and bringing to them the full light of the gospel. They would be just as painfully blinded as I was. For me to avoid that pain, I had to ask my friends to make a big noise as they were approaching the meeting point so that if I got there first and may have fallen asleep, I could wake up and gradually readjust to the light. For them, a little of the light of the gospel at a time would be the best way to eventually receive and embrace in deep understanding the full meaning of the redemption Christ has offered them.

CAVE PHOTOGRAPHY

Taking good pictures in caves is not an easy task and requires a lot of patience, good equipment, and lots of knowledge. Even with the most powerful flashes, large voids cannot be photographed. The very high humidity of the cave atmosphere increases the absorption of light. There are also problems when using film because of the use of artificial light sources (which change the colors on natural light films) so that filters are needed which reduce the film speed. The use of artificial light films on the other hand is not the best because when using only flashes, unpleasant colors result unless filters are again used. With the advent of high-resolution digital cameras, a simple setting on a button solves all of these problems. True SLR digital cameras are needed though because the "B" ("Bulb") function is used to allow the shutter to be kept open for as long as the photographer wants.

That is because the vast majority of cave photographs (except for some snapshots) are taken from a tripod and some can take up to an hour to be properly lit. Before taking a picture, the photographer needs to study the shot. Standing in the most favorable spot, he/she will ask colleagues to move around the chamber or section of the chamber that will be immortalized, repeatedly asking for the light sources to be moved until the best effects are obtained. He/she then needs to memorize those angles and proceed with the shot very much like a film director does with his actors. In the first stage, the "actors" (more like walking light sources in fact) — the more of them the better — are waiting on their locations and trigger the light source (usually a flash or a halogen source) in the direction requested by the "director." The photographer then covers the lenses of his camera (this is where a stable tripod comes in really handy) and asks his colleagues to move to the next location. If the lenses are not covered, then as they move, their light sources will leave all sorts of undesired "graphics" in the picture. Once in the new location, the lighting is resumed, and so on until the desired lighting is achieved.

This is, however, a delicate issue; only experienced photographers are able to know when to close the shutter so that enough light and darkness is "stored." When large voids are photographed, leaving unlit or grayish areas alternating with well-lit ones is essential to render the depth and mystery of the place. Interesting effects can be obtained from such an elaborate setup, like having the same person at various locations in the same picture, or when subtly using light, a person's contour can be more or less melted into the background. The use of digital cameras (though not many of them are reliable enough for prolonged use in the harsh, equipment-unfriendly cave environment) has made photography easier as one can check the quality of the picture after taking it. I remember the old days when my heart was pounding as I was washing my slide films after having developed them and rolled them out to see how many of the 36 shots were acceptable.

Photographers often use added lights to enhance a cave's beauty, as seen in these photographs.

CHAPTER SIX

STUDYING CAVES

If one wants to understand caves, one needs to study not only the terrains that host them (karstlands) but also the adjacent ones, including the climate and the vegetation. This is why the study of caves became a broader interdisciplinary approach referred to as karstology (in Europe where it was born) or karst science (in North America where it has just "arrived"). Karst is seen in karstology as a system with inputs (essentially the acidic water), the throughput (normally a "black box," but in the case of caves a "grey box" because parts of it can be seen by humans) represented by the host (karstic) rock and all that happens inside it in order for the inputs to arrive at the other end as outputs, essentially saturated or unsaturated water.

Once penetrated into the rock through the cave systems, water can simply transit without any significant change in chemical proprieties, only cooling or warming (depending on the season and/or the geographic position), or it will use its acidity to attack whatever soluble rocks it may come in contact with. The cave walls (including ceiling and floor) are the primary target. Breakdown blocks (from the walls and/or ceiling) are also subject to dissolution as are speleothems.

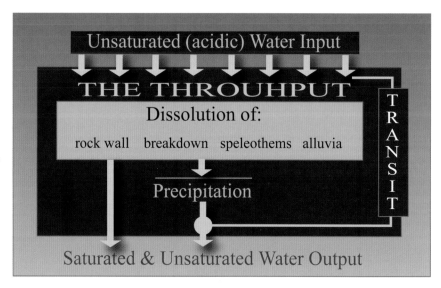

Karst geosystem

Karren, Innerbergli karst terrain, Switzerland

years) across a horizontal surface. This, however, refers only to chemical erosion (solutional erosion) while mechanical erosion (e.g., river erosion, roots breaking up the rock, freeze and thaw [cryoclasty], etc.) is left out. This is why karst denudation is a very relative parameter, especially when extrapolated over longer periods of time. Nobody has measured the removal of karst rock for 1,000 years, though, so all actually measured values are necessarily extrapolated over that period of time. Obviously, that assumes a constant (uniform) denudation rate, but nothing is really uniform in karst.

When the water infiltrates (essentially by capillary flow) the rock via cracks, joints, and bedding planes (i.e., non-karstic conduits), basically all the water acidity is consumed on the enlargement of these access routes. This would be the only way in which karst conduits could be generated. Obviously, all of the dissolved calcite will be carried toward the final destination, which in this case cannot be the emergence of the waters through karst springs because there would be no continuous connection to the exit point yet. Thousands of measurements around the world have shown that most of the acidic water infiltrating into karst rocks is neutralized (loses its acidity) within the first 32 feet (10 m) below the surface. If it is to penetrate farther, acidic water must be continuously resupplied, but that is impossible within capillary conduits! Imagine a V-shaped capillary fissure (as the vast majority of them actually are). The acidic water at its tip, once

If there are any soluble particles in the alluvia — and in caves there are a lot of those — they will also be subject to dissolution. Once the water is saturated, it will simply transit the remainder of the cave without dissolving any more rock. In some cases, the flowing water will actually precipitate a part of its mineral load (calcite essentially) in the streambed itself. This could cause the gravel there to be cemented so that a thin layer of conglomerate may form. Because the water acidity works on so many different targets, the rate at which cave walls are dissolved is not very high (unless none of the alternative items listed above are present). Therefore, one cannot just measure the amount of dissolved calcite in a karst outlet during a year and hence estimate how quickly caves form, because it is impossible to know how much of the dissolved calcite in the outflowing waters of karst systems comes only from the dissolution of the bedrock. The only measurement of the karsting processes generally accepted is the karst denudation rate, expressed in millimeters per millennium and representing the thickness of rock (in millimeters) removed per unit of time (1,000

it is neutralized, must be replaced by new acidic water, but the only way to do that is by removing (displacing) it and that requires high pressures that are never achieved inside the karstic rocks. Therefore, whatever acidic water reaches greater depths can only get there via pre-existing proper karst conduits (i.e., larger than capillary cracks, joints, and faults). As for the saturated water, whenever it reaches a larger void, the sudden depressurizing (loss of CO_2) will cause the precipitation of calcite and growth of speleothems. Without the CO_2, on the other hand, this water is not acidic anymore.

All of the above leave the usual long-age (evolutionary) model of cave/karst formation in a difficult situation. In order for caves to form by infiltrating water charged with CO_2, it has to postulate pre-existing conduits (i.e., a previous karsting of a different type).

We will see later that such a karsting can be consistent with the Bible.

From a strictly scientific point of view, caves are natural sections through rock units. Oftentimes, they also provide direct access to the karst water table, thus replacing information from boreholes at a fraction of the cost. The study of caves covers many different areas of science. Subterranean geomorphology is the very first, as it deals with the complex morphologies encountered under the ground and their relationships with the surface morphologies. Geology is another area of investigation, from the survey of all formations (hard rocks and sediments) encountered to tectonics (faults, folds, etc.). Geochemistry also has its place under the ground, as the scientist has direct access to many different types of rocks and their direct chemical interactions with the environment. As a result of that interaction, each rock leaves a " chemical signature" which covers an area larger than the rock itself does, and water is the carrier of that signature. Hydrology is obviously a major part of cave studies because it helps in understanding how waters move or are stored in the rocks. Hydrogeology combines hydrology, geology, and chemistry into a complex analysis of the rock-water interaction, providing an in-depth understanding of, and valuable information about, the size and quality of water reserves.

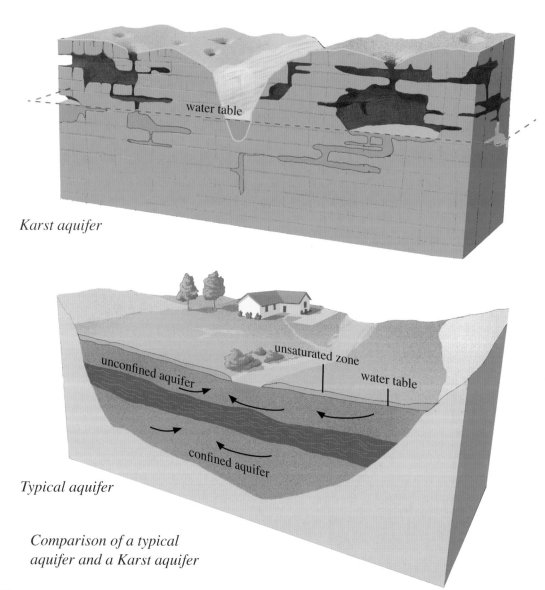

Karst aquifer

Typical aquifer

Comparison of a typical aquifer and a Karst aquifer

STUDYING THE SURFACE

As mentioned before, the surface karst features are a reflection of the subterranean ones and they are closely related. This is why when investigating karstlands, investigation should first be directed at what happens to the waters that reach the karstic rocks. There are two basic types of such waters: the precipitation water and the fluvial water (carried by streams or rivers). A part of the runoff evaporates after it reaches the ground. That can be measured in various areas and a total (average, in fact) evaporation percentage can be calculated for a certain area. The total flow of the existing surface streams can also be measured and that essentially represents the amount of rain that does not evaporate and does not infiltrate into karstic rocks. On the other hand, the total average amount of precipitation (rain and snow) can be measured quite accurately. If the sum of the evaporation and stream flow is below that average amount of precipitation, the difference is represented by infiltration (loss to the rocks). To know how much of that infiltration is in karst, one more thing needs to be measured: the sum of all karst outputs (karst springs). Usually that comes very close to the amount of missing water. All of the above measurements represent the water budget of a given area. Properly understanding the water budget of a karst area and its surroundings is essential to a proper understanding of karst.

Once the water budget is completed (and that takes a minimum of one full year, but in most cases several years of recordings), the study of karst requires knowing as much as possible about the subterranean routes the karst waters follow. This is achieved by tracing: Sinking streams are dyed (with a harmless dye) or injected with other various resilient tracers. All outlets (karst springs) are then monitored for emerging dye or tracers. When they eventually emerge, tracers can provide a wealth of information: how quickly water moves underground, if there are subterranean confluences (a sinking stream merges with other sinking streams), if there are vast amounts of stored water, how karst aquifers respond to rains, etc. Extremely valuable information is yielded by continuous measurements of the discharge or flow rates (hydrograph) and chemical composition (chemograph) of waters emerging through karst springs. Flow and chemistry are a direct function of how well or how poorly a subterranean drainage is organized.

Once water tracing is accomplished, the surface is thoroughly surveyed (often karst features are incorrectly represented on topographic maps or they are not present at all because the topographers have no understanding of karst relief). The layout of many surface features (like aligned sinkholes) provides valuable information on the subterranean features.

STUDYING THE SYSTEM

With all the available information on the surface and subsurface at hand, karstologists proceed with the most important part of karst studies: modeling the respective karst aquifers. If we understand how they function and respond to surface events, we can make good and sustainable use of their water resources.

Though far from being completely understood, the karst aquifer (or karst system) is viewed today as a transport and storage device. Water travels from the surface through minute conduits (cracks, joints, faults) toward two destinations: a main conduit — the drain — and a vast array of voids adjacent to the drain — the annexes.

At flood flow (high waters), a part of the water surplus is sent, even "pumped" into the annexes. At normal flow, most of the water infiltrating flows through the drain. At baseflow (lowest flow), a part of the water stored in the annexes is supplied to the drain so that its flow is maintained at a fairly regular rate, unlike any other type of aquifer. Only after extensive droughts does the flow of a major karst spring significantly decrease. This is why karst springs are some of the most reliable water sources.

Many of these elements have been discovered during the many years in which the Baget karst system, in the Pyrenees, in France, has been thoroughly investigated. It is interesting how, in the case of the Baget karst aquifer, tiny aquatic creatures — copepods — have significantly contributed to the understanding of that aquifer. The life cycle of the copepods is well understood and it was observed repeatedly that after significant floods, which expel large numbers of adult copepods through the main drain, adults kept emerging a few days later as if nothing had happened. Since months are needed for new adults to grow, the only possible source for more adults would have been the annexes (which acted

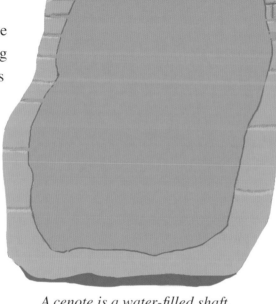

A cenote is a water-filled shaft.

as buffers and therefore were not forcibly drained). Coupled with a short recharge time, this information has provided enough evidence not only for the reality of the annexes but also of their major role in karst aquifer storage.

In the Yucatan province of Mexico, the heartland of the ancient Maya, lie many entrances to what the Mayans called Xibalba — the "Underworld." They are called cenotes, bell-shaped shafts with deep lakes at the bottom, sort of like water-filled sinkholes. One near the ancient town

A cenote in the Yucatan Penninsula, Mexico

of Cichén Itzá ("Cenote of Sacrifice") received the slain bodies of many humans as offerings to the gods. The city was in fact built around many such cenotes. The surface of the lakes inside cenotes represents the regional karst water table, which makes them a form of annex open to the surface.

HAZARDS IN KARSTLANDS

As mentioned before, karst aquifers provide a significant part of the drinking water for human populations worldwide and they are expected to provide even more in the near future. The knowledge we now have of them allows a sustainable use but is not adequate when it comes to constructions in karst terrains. The drain and annexes represent the big picture, but the detailed structure cannot really be known. Theoretically, whatever void is located below the water table should be water-filled. Yet that is only valid if that void is connected through conduits to the karst aquifer. Here is one characteristic case: a subterranean hydropower plant was planned in karstlands in Romania, over 320 feet (100 m) below the local water table. A borehole was drilled in the axis of the shaft that was to open access to the area where a huge underground chamber was planned. The borehole encountered many small voids without any significant water flow and the 19.6-foot (6 m) diameter shaft was subsequently dug to 347 feet (106 m) deep, with repeated test boreholes fanning downward. Still no significant flows were intercepted. Once the projected depth was attained, lateral

blasting followed, in order to begin the chamber excavation in earnest. After the third blast, water gushed into the mining works, forcing evacuation. Within less than three days the shaft was flooded up to 11.4 feet (3.5 m) below the rim, the depth corresponding to the local karst water table! The geologists responsible for this work made the mistake of ignoring the characteristics of karst aquifers, following poorly defined standards (designed for non-karstic areas). They did not extend the proof drilling far enough and had not previously investigated the basic karst features in the area.

Karstologists would never recommend any significant mining activities below the karst water table. And that is also valid for dams built on limestones and other karstic rocks. Even with all the special precautions in regard to karst, many such dams have still failed to perform their task for the projected time frame. Water always found its way through karst aquifers, draining away from the artificial water reservoirs. In fact, the increased pressure of accumulating water almost always accelerates karsting processes, and cases have been recorded of water emerging from deep below a dam within less than five years!

Cenote of Sacrifice, Chichen Itza, Yucatan, Mexico. Natives of this area were known to sacrifice human beings by throwing them into the cenote.

CAVE CONSERVATION

With more and more humans entering caves for either leisure or science, cave protection has become a serious issue in recent years. Cavers have a saying: "Take nothing but pictures, leave nothing but memories, kill nothing but time." Unfortunately, the thrill of discovery and the sheer adventure nowadays attract many individuals for whom caves are merely a special sports arena and a place to pick up souvenirs. One of the best ways to protect caves is to keep their location unknown to the public. Another rather drastic one is to gate caves and limit access to reliable individuals and under adequate guidance. Many caves have such a scientific value, like the painted caves in southern France and northern Spain, that opening them to visits would be extremely dangerous for the treasures they host. It appears that the carbon dioxide added by the visitors' breathing increases the speed at which speleothems form. In cases like Niaux Cave, new speleothems started growing in the middle of ancient drawings! (See photo below.) In the case of the famous Lascaux Cave in France, exact copies of the paintings have been made in another nearby cave, offering visitors a near-real experience.

Karstlands themselves are one of the most sensitive types of environments because what happens on the surface has a significant effect on what happens under the ground. In other terrains, water infiltrates slowly into the rocks and needs a long time to travel through them. In karstlands, however, infiltration can be extremely fast. In many cases, infiltrating water can reach the caves within hours or even minutes after reaching the soil! Some of the older cottages built high up on the karstlands in southern France (in the Pyrenees) discharged their sewerage into potholes and the contents were found to be draining into several caves. In remote rural areas in Romania, *E. coli* infections of cattle were found to be due to domestic pollution from communities upstream of caves that drain sinking streams; the cattle regularly drank the water coming from the caves.

One particular discovery has highlighted not only the sensitivity of karstlands to pollution but also the exquisite archive that caves represent. Studying the radioactive fallout of the Chernobyl nuclear reactor accident, the artificial radioisotopes ^{134}Cs and ^{137}Cs were

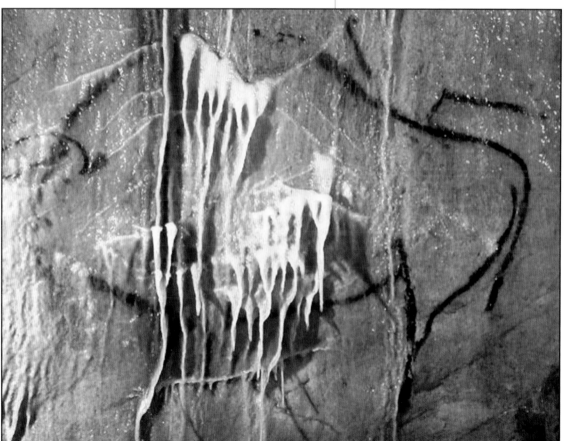

In Niaux Cave, speleothems started growing in the middle of ancient drawings!

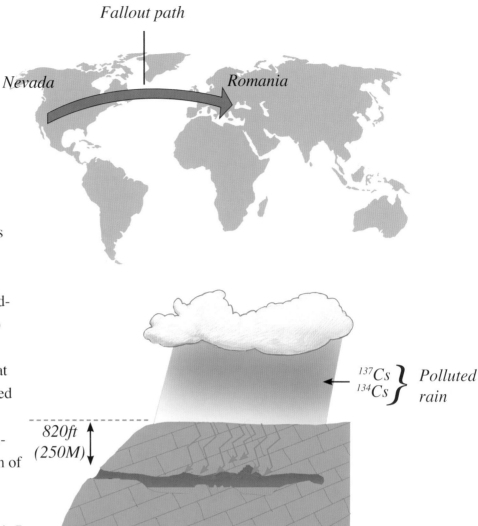

Fallout path

Nevada   Romania

^{137}Cs ^{134}Cs } *Polluted rain*

820ft (250M)

ound in the sediments on the ottom of a 40-foot (12 m) deep ke in the cave Ghețarul de sub gurăşti in Romania in 1995 ess than 620 miles [1,000 km] om the accident site). This lake over 1,300 horizontal feet (400) from the cave entrance and 820 ertical feet (250 m) below the urface. The radioisotopes took less an a year to infiltrate and reach e bottom of the lake. Deeper in e sediments, in a layer correspond- g to the year 1963, ^{137}Cs was also ound. That year, the only possible ource was the atmospheric blasts at e Nevada nuclear site in the United tates, half a world away! Once gain, the ^{137}Cs-carrying water infil- ated the cave, reaching the bottom of e lake in less than one year.

THE FORMATION OF KARST

As mentioned before, the formation of aves in the evolutionary view takes tens r hundreds of thousands of years. Yet ven for that evolutionist need pre- xisting conduits, which means that there ad to be a different way to form caves. ike, for example, the one in the Guadalupe Moun- ins described before. There is also another type of arsting due to ascending hot solutions (hydrothermal arsting) that, like the sulfuric acid karst in the Guada- pe Mountains, is considered an exception to the rule. ut was it so in the past? Let us consider an alterna- ve karsting model.

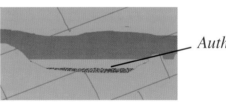

Authigenic clay and silt

Creationary model of cave formation

THE CREATIONARY MODEL

Naturalistic science claims to have found alleged ancient karst features in some of the oldest known rocks, but those features can easily be interpreted as the result of processes other than karsting.

The Genesis flood was a global catastrophe of a magnitude and intensity this planet has never witnessed before or since. In order to visualize its phenomenal effect on the rocks, landscape, climate, and living creatures, one should first get rid of all biases based on known geological phenomena. Most of the processes involved in the Flood, though a number

Stages of rock formation

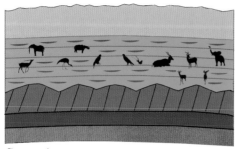

Stage 1

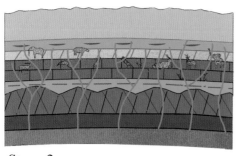

Stage 2

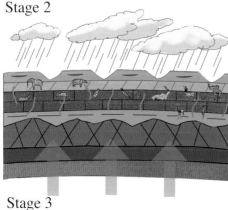

Stage 3

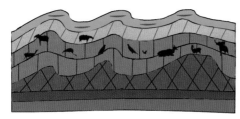

Stage 4

occur today, were of a scale and intensity that cannot be compared with anything known nowadays.

FORMATION OF THE ROCKS

One of the main results of the Flood was a tremendous amount of soft sediments accumulating everywhere, in the ocean basins and on the newly formed continents (broken up from a single landmass or supercontinent) still submerged during the Flood. Most of these sediments were made of particles originating from pre-Flood rocks, including larger chunks of coral reefs and their associated ecosystems. As a result of massive changes deep inside the earth, tremendous amounts of hot and chemically hyperactive solutions (generically called "hydrothermal") rose toward the flooded crust, intensely circulating through the soft, waterlogged sediments. The hydrothermal solutions themselves contained large amounts of calcite. Even today, solutions coming from deep inside the crust discharge calcite on the bottom of the ocean like in the case of the Lost City hot vent in the Northern Atlantic where a 60-foot high mound of calcite has built up.

Complex chemical reactions resulted between the sediments, the water in them, and those hot solutions. In places, parts of the coral reefs (and other rocks formed of carbonates — predominantly calcium carbonate or calcite) were dissolved so that more calcite was added to the mineral load of the solutions.

In other places, the calcite precipitated between the grains of the soft sediments, binding them together like a cement (matrix), thus creating hard rocks (through a process geologists call diagenesis). Whenever calcite was predominant, limestones resulted.

FORMATION OF THE CAVES

In the later stages of the Flood, many of the hydrothermal solutions became unsaturated and therefore ready to dissolve more rock. Limestone was the most susceptible to this. While still buried deep inside the newly formed sedimentary cover (even before it emerged from the sea, at the end of the Flood), unsaturated solutions started dissolving it, wherever they reached it. In places this was as an intricate maze of conduits, in other places as more or less straight pipes.

At the end of the Flood, as the continents were emerging from the sea and mountains were being rapidly built, many of these conduits were lifted above the sea and rivers. Therefore, the fluids in them tended to drain toward the sea or the nearest rivers. On the other hand, at this time the limestone, initially still plastic, folded. Later, as it became hard, it broke along fault lines, cracks, and joints. Obviously, wherever conduits existed inside the rock, the faults and other smaller break lines would preferentially follow them.

Faulting, and rapid erosion by the receding flood waters, opened many of these fluid-filled conduits, draining them. Thus the first caves were opened to the surface. After the Flood, the climate on earth was drastically different, as the distribution of the continents and the dynamics of the ocean drastically changed because of the Flood. Massive precipitation poured down for many years. Like any rain that falls, a part of it infiltrated the rocks via faults and cracks. Inside limestones,

A CREATIONARY MODEL FOR CAVE FORMATION

As soft sediments began diagenesis (turning sediments into rock) hyperactive hydrothermal solutions rising from inside the earth rapidly dissolved large, maze-like voids in the soluable rocks. They were filled with fluids and insoluble residues.

Stage 1

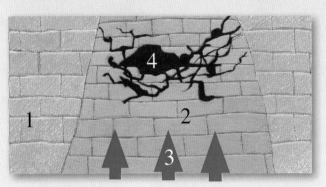

1. *Insoluble rocks*
2. *Soluable rocks (limestone, dolostone, rock gypsum)*
3. *Hyperactive hydrothermal solutions generated during the Flood*
4. *Large karst cavities excavated immediately after diagenis*

Stage 2

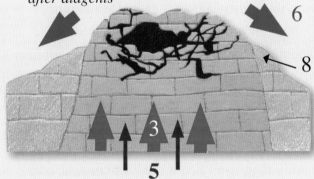

5. *Global tectonic uplift*
6. *Global sheet flow (Flood water receding)*
7. *Massive rain*
8. *New, detrital sediments*

Stage 3

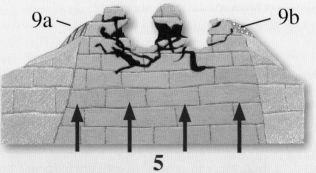

9. *Karstic sediments a) travertine (tufa); b) debris cone*

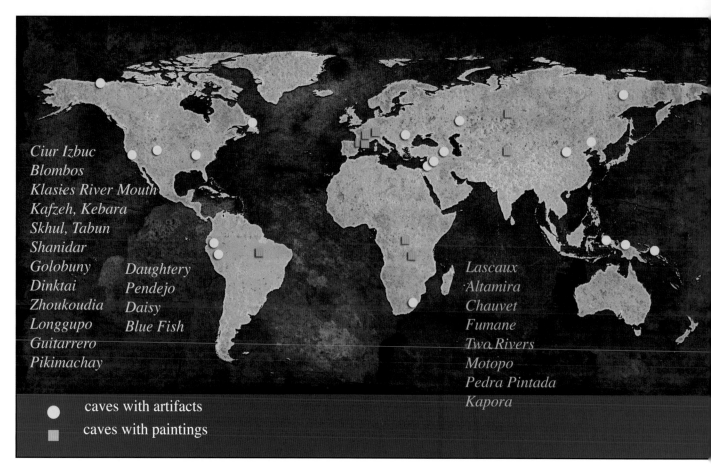

Ciur Izbuc
Blombos
Klasies River Mouth
Kafzeh, Kebara
Skhul, Tabun
Shanidar
Golobuny   Daughtery
Dinktai   Pendejo
Zhoukoudia   Daisy
Longgupo   Blue Fish
Guitarrero
Pikimachay

Lascaux
Altamira
Chauvet
Fumane
Two Rivers
Motopo
Pedra Pintada
Kapora

● caves with artifacts
■ caves with paintings

however, the infiltrating water encountered numerous conduits and other types of voids created by the hydrothermal solutions. These rapidly became subterranean drainages, like a huge regional sewer system! The presence of many decomposing organic remains on the surface of the rocks (as the Flood waters receded) dramatically increased the amount of carbon dioxide in the infiltrating rainwater, which increased the acidity. As a consequence, the limestone was further dissolved (much faster than it is today). The conduits were rapidly reshaped and they began to look like the caves we are used to today. Speleothems rapidly grew as the precipitation rates continued to stay high. These were the heydays of cave reshaping and decoration!

Then, within about 500 years after the Flood, the Ice Age stepped in, as a result of the massive precipitation in the higher latitudes (which was mostly snow). The freezing in the soil (permafrost), the sealing of many cave entrances by the ice sheets, and the smaller amounts of fluid water in general negatively influenced

cave formation from further enlargement of passages to speleothem growth. It was also during this time that, under the pressure of the increasingly hostile climate, many animals and humans started looking for shelter inside caves, subsequently leaving remains and artifact in many of them.

The earliest human habitation (according to evolutionary anthropology) of caves occurred in China (Longgupo Cave), which has the largest surface of karstlands in the world. It is reasonable to assume that the first caves available to humans would have been located where the largest number of caves could form, and that is indeed in China.

While the land was still covered by the ice sheets, tremendous amounts of meltwater accumulated below them, bursting repeatedly as massive local or regional floods that have scoured the land. The caves under the ice sheets suffered repeated floods, often resulting in partial or complete clogging of passages with gravel, sand, and clay. Subsequently, as these sediments were aterlogged, some caves drained catastrophically, with ome sediments still left behind. It is common nowaays to find gravel, sand, and clay hanging on ledges in he walls of cave passages and not at all uncommon to nd whole side passages still filled to the top with the ame sediments. As the Ice Age began to recede a few housand years ago (the rather large extent of glaciers oday shows that the Ice Age is not completely finished; or 85 percent of the earth's age, all scientists agree, he average temperature of the planet was substantially varmer than today), tremendous amounts of meltwater vashed the land, often as regional floods like the Misoula Flood, which is known to have carved the famous Channeled Scablands.[5] In karstlands, this excess of water has significantly enlarged and reshaped many caves. Many speleothems were ripped off and buried in sediments (where some are still present today). New speleothems also formed very quickly as large amounts of water were available. Furthermore, this water was more chemically aggressive because of the cold. The colder he water, the more carbon dioxide it can contain,

therefore, the more limestone that will be dissolved and moved away to supply new speleothems.

The landscape was substantially reshaped by the ice and meltwater, so that in many cases cave passages that used to drain water became dry, and the ones that used to be flooded (saturated) beneath them now became drains. Relieved from the burden of ice, the land rebounded upward and many slopes readjusted to the positions of the new valleys. The rapid erosion associated with this has oftentimes obliterated old cave entrances and opened new ones. So, many of the old accesses (used by some cave dwellers) were destroyed.

Forests have grown where once the land was covered by ice, and their roots and the whole ecosystem associated with them have started to supply more carbon dioxide into the infiltrating water, thus keeping speleothems alive. By and large, what we see today unfolding in karstlands is a slow re-shaping of features formed in the past during entirely different climatic and hydraulic (water movement) conditions. Everything is slowed down today, so that it is wrong to assume that the pace at which karsting (surface features, cave and speleothem formation) processes unfold today was the same in the past. Therefore, any attempt to estimate the ages of caves (and karst in general), based on present processes, is incorrect. So far from contradicting the account of the Book of Genesis in any way, karst is actually largely a result of the conditions existing at the end of the Genesis flood.

Caves are a very special environment in which God's wonderful work awaits us in the darkness only to reveal something of His grandeur and infinite wisdom. The fact that beauty can be stored in absolute darkness, and only becomes accessible to humans after significant effort (and often risk) brings to mind a beautiful passage from the Scripture: "If I say, 'Surely the darkness will overwhelm me and the light around me will be night,' even the darkness is not dark to You, and the night is as bright as the day. Darkness and light are alike to You" (Psalm 139:11–12).

Archaeological excavation of a site at the Lazaret caves in southern France. These caves have yielded a wide range of early human artifacts.

Many troglophile creatures that die in caves are given a traditional cave burial, being covered by calcite. Bats (as individuals, groups or large colonies) often hang close to speleothems and when some die and come to rest in a dripping zone, like the top of a stalagmite, they are soon covered by calcite. This bat (in the photo below) has some preserved tissue besides bones, evidence it was covered rather quickly.

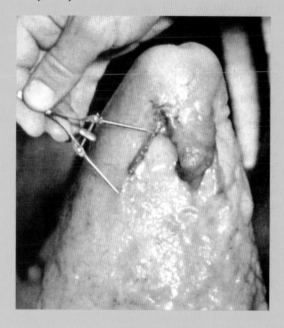

There are many other examples of not only animals but also a variety of man-made items that show rapid covering by calcite in caves; consider the following account: "Among the photos that Max Porter (Virginia, USA) sent of objects encapsulated by rapid growth of cave formations in Virginia's Shenandoah Valley was this one. Max recounted how the cave guides had repeatedly espoused the official line that stalactites and stalagmites are very old. So when Max saw this crock (butter churn?) along a walkway in Endless Caverns, he questioned the tour guide as to how many 'millions of years' it had taken to almost totally encapsulate the crock. The guide replied, 'Oh, that sits under an overactive stalactite.' Apparently the crock had been left there around 85 years ago to collect dripping water for the workers to drink while constructing pathways for public access. As Max says, it didn't need millions of years, just the right conditions."[6]

The limestone blocks of this basement (below) have provided the bulk of the calcite dissolved by acidic water infiltrating from the surface.

Caves in the United States

A Little Glimpse at the Many Skills and Talents It Takes to Explore Caves

Having only spent the last few years in North America, my photo archive of North American karst is rather limited. My friend Mike Liston has graciously helped with the following pictures and comments.

The author in his "laboratory" and secondary home

It takes a great deal of training to do vertical rope work above ground, let alone in a hostile enviroment like that which you find underground.

It takes a very competent person to do it safely in the daylight. Now throw in water and mud, maybe even some ice. Add to this the fact that you are cold and tired, quite likely hungry.

You are dragging not only yourself through this cave, but also your equipment and delicate photographic equipment. All of this is done in order to share with the outside world your many discoveries.

Vertical rope work training, before going into a vertical shaft

The bonds formed between team members during such trying and difficult times are some of the strongest around.

The tight crawls, cold and wet conditions, bone-numbing tiredness, and mind-dizzying vertical drops you may be exposed to all bring you face to face with your own human limitations.

You tend to come away from the experience a stronger more confident person, yet more humble and honest about yourself.

Descent into the Devil's Graveyard Cave, Indiana. The cable ladder can be used in many ways, according to the spelunker's skills and confidence.

A tight squeeze in Sweckers Stream Cave, West Virgina

FUN IN THE MUD

Part of what makes cave exploring fun is to be able to share this unique part of God's Creation with youth groups. Besides! It is just plain clean (real muddy), wholesome fun!

Youth groups tend to be pumped up with excitement after experiencing a wild cave trip for the first time. Their parents are not there to take care of them, and they are forced to learn to depend on one another and also that they can accomplish so much more when they work together as a team. It builds great confidence!

What better way for a young person to truly learn about God's Creation than to go explore inside it?

One particular passage in Biehle's Cave, Indiana, is full of what is called "liquid mud" and these youth enjoyed the experience so much that they insisted on crawling back in the cave, in order to swim their way, through the mud and back out again!

A subterranean stream cutting through the bedrock inside a cave is very confined (as compared to a surface stream that can easily move in search of the ideal flow path). So instead of meandering only on a horizontal plane, a subterranean stream sometimes meanders in a vertical plane also. The result is such usually a vertical succession of ledges (convexities) and corresponding niches (concavities).

Vertical meandering in Ellison's Cave, Georgia

It is amazing to see the eagerness and desire to learn more about what God has created, after a group of new cavers have crawled up out of a hole in the ground.

The youth seem to enjoy getting muddy; the dirtier the better! It is like wearing a badge of honor to them. It seems to be that girls have a tendency to want to "share" (smear) the mud they have with anyone close enough to touch.

GEOLOGICAL PROCESSES

Water takes and water gives. It takes away the limestone by dissolving it and later and elsewhere, "remorseful," it gives back the essence of the limestone (pure calcite) in myriad shapes, colors, and textures.

Resonance Cave, B.C., Canada, a phreatic tube controlled by a bedding plane.

In some caves a very stable climate and a constant supply of saturated water make calcite grow freely and unimpressed by gravity. The results are often spectacular, like the famous "Butterfly" in the Caverns of Sonora, Texas.

Ellison's Cave is full of many and varied processes that could lead to rapid cave formation. It is also a prime example of a "hypogene" cave, meaning its origins began from below, rather being formed from the top down by water percolating down through the earth. It shows evidence of forming from below, quite possibly from "hydrothermal" waters, containing large amounts of hydrogen sulfide.

When limestone (calcium carbonate) is exposed to sulfuric acid, it forms gypsum which is calcium sulfate with two water molecules. Calcium sulfate alone is known as "anhydrite."

The walls and floors of Ellison's Cave are crusted with gypsum!

The photos at left are examples of horizontal bedding planes. Some of them are huge, thick layers of the same consistency, 15 feet thick! Anyone who works with concrete can tell you that you would have to pour such a layer very quickly indeed in order to achieve the same results.

If you wait and let one layer of the cement set up, or mix a new batch, and pour it, then the mixture is ever so slightly different, and it leaves a new distinct layer.

And yet we are told that limestones are laid down over the centuries at the bottom of the ocean by the slow process of calcite from sea shells settling and drifting down.

A much better "event" comes to my mind. That of a colossal cement truck pouring out massive bed of limestone. Or better yet, a catostrophic worldwide flood.

Gypsum formations in the Tilt Table Room, Ellison's Cave, Georgia

Gypsum on cave walls. Ellison's Cave, Georgia

While the exploration and study of caves can be an exciting challenge, it is can also be a very dangerous one which should only be left to professionals and trained explorers. Visit local commercially-operated caves in your area, and if you want to develop skills in cave exploration, become part of trained professional groups in your area. Never explore alone, unprepared, or without the proper skills, equipment, and following all of the needed safety procedures.

Photo Credits

References

1. A. Leroi-Gourhan, *Prehistoire de l'art occidental*. (Paris: Editions d'art Lucien Mazenod, 1971).

2. J.D. Lewis-Williams, "*Southern African Archaeology in the 1990s*," *African Archaeological Bulletin* 48 (1993): p. 49.

3. Dr. Gheorghe Racoviţă, the grandson of Emil G. Racoviţă, founder of biospeleology and the world's first speleological institute.

4. A.P. Krueger and E.J. Reed, "Biological Impact of Small Ions," Science 193 (1976): p. 1209–13.
   This mechanism most likely arose after the Flood, and as a consequence of it.

5. M.J. Oard, *The Missoula Flood Controversy and the Genesis Flood*. (Chino Valley, AZ: Creation Research Society, 2004).

6. "Young Crock, Young Rock," *Creation* 27, no. 4 (September-November 2005): 5.

Glossary

Anthodite: flower-like ("anthos" in Greek meaning "flower") gypsum speleothem.

Aragonite: calcium carbonate crystallizing in the orthorhombic system, slightly denser and with less a visible cleavage than calcite.

Autochthonous: local, having formed where it's found today.

Base level: the lowest level a river can cut down. For karst it is the lowest (in terms of elevation) river that drains a karst aquifer.

Blind valley: a valley that ends abruptly at the foot of an escarpment.

Blowing cave: a cave with a continuous air current.

Calcite: calcium carbonate ($CaCO_3$) crystallizing in the trigonal (rhombohedral) system. It is the main constituent of limestones and speleothems.

Cave pearls: rounded (very rarely angular) concretion formed by precipitation of calcite (rarely aragonite) around a nucleus (usually a rock fragment).

Cave rafts: a thin mineral film, usually of calcite, floating on a cave pool. When it becomes too thick, it breaks into flakes and sinks to the bottom of the pool.

Ceiling pocket: solution cavity on the ceiling of a cave, shaped like the interior of a kettle.

Cenote: steep-walled natural well reaching the water table and continuing below it.

Chemotrophic: a food chain in which the base has a metabolism based on chemical energy rather than light (phototrophic).

Column: the fusion of a stalactite and a stalagmite.

Denudation rate: the pace at which a given surface of bare rock is eroded. Usually measured in millimeters per millennium (thousand years).

Desiccation cracks: cracks occurring because of shrinking of sediment as it dries.

Diagenesis: a complex set of transformations through which sediments go, from compaction, through dewatering to cementation.

Dissociation: breaking down of a solid into particles by a solvent in which the solid preserves its chemical composition. Salt dissolved in water is still salt (NaCl).

Dissolution: breaking down of a solid by a solvent into molecules in which the solid's chemical composition changes. Calcite ($CaCO_3$) dissolved in water becomes $Ca(HCO_3)_2$.

Doline: Synonym for sinkholes in Europe and most of the karstological literature.

Dolomitization: a chemical process through which solutions circulating through carbonate sediments add magnesium to calcite transforming it into dolomite, $CaMg(CO_3)_2$.

Eccentrics: very pure calcite crystals often growing "against gravity" (i.e., not controlled by a dripping point).

Emergence: the place where subterranean waters emerge to the surface.

Endogenetic: caused by forces/processes originating inside (the earth in this case).

Evaporite rocks (and karst): rocks formed by evaporation of water and precipitation of its mineral content, like rock gypsum and rock salt.

Exogenetic: caused by forces/processes outside (the earth in this case).

Geochemistry: a branch of geology and chemistry investigating the chemical composition of the rocks as well as the processes that cause and control chemical changes in rocks.

Geosystem: the assembly of rocks and processes that create and transform them.

Helictite: twisted, often-times spiraling calcite formation hanging from the ceiling or walls of a cave passage.

Heligmite: a helictite growing on the floor of a cave passage.

Hydrogeology: branch of science investigating the interactions between rocks and water.

Hydrograph: the continuous recording (graphic or digital) of selected properties of a body of water (usually river).

Hydrothermal: a domain within rocks in which warm to hot solutions ascending from inside the earth chemically affect the rocks or/and deposit minerals in voids.

Insurgence: a point (sometimes area) where surface waters sink underground.

Karren: channels or furrows dissolved by water on bare limestone.

Karst: the term used by scientists to describe a landscape of caverns, sinking streams, sinkholes, and a vast array of small-scale features all generated by the solution of the bedrock, formed predominantly by limestones.

Karst aquifer: the assembly of ground water accumulated inside a karstic rock, enough to supply wells and springs.

Karst relief: the assembly of landforms generated by solution of karstic rocks.

Karstic rocks: soluble rocks on which most landforms are formed by solution (karren, sinkholes, blind valleys, swallets, uvalas, poljes, etc.)

Karst spring: a spring discharging a karst aquifer.

Karsting: the complex process of forming karst relief.

Karstology: interdisciplinary science analyzing karstlands as a system with all its elements (autochthonous and allochthonous) integrated in a holistic approach.

Kyr: kilo years (i.e., thousands of years).

Limestone pavement: karren, usually in regular patterns, extending on large surfaces.

Master joint: a tectonic discontinuity (fault line) that a given cave passage follows.

Mirabilite: a rare cave mineral consisting of sodium sulphate needing ten molecules of water to create a crystalline structure ($Na_2SO_4 \bullet 10H_2O$).

Meroclimate: a "micro-micro climate" (i.e., a given area of a cave where temperature and humidity are relatively constant) with amplitudes (i.e., difference between the highest and lowest) not in excess of 2°C.

Microclimate: a small geographic area (like a valley or several adjacent valleys) where climate is significantly different from the regional one.

Moonmilk: a pasty (plastic) mass of precipitated milkish white carbonates of calcium and/or magnesium (hydrocarbonates). The consistency varies from soft cream to ice cream.

Orthokarst: karst formed on carbonate rocks mainly by solution.

Parakarst: karst-like features formed on non-carbonate rocks, mainly by solution.

Phreatic caves: flooded (water-saturated) caves formed and/or located below the water table.

Pocket valley: a valley that starts suddenly at the foot of an escarpment that closes a gorge.

Polje: a large (sometimes over 100 km long) flat-bottomed, sediment-lined depression (hollow) surrounded by steep mountains. It can have one or several streams/rivers emerging from karst springs and sinking into a swallow holes or ponors.

Ponor: the original Slovenian word for a place where a river or stream sinks into the ground. (Synonym: swallow hole or swallet.)

Pseudokarst: Karst-like features formed on any kind of rock by other ways than solution.

Resurgence: the place where a sinking stream re-emerges to the surface.

Rimstone: wall-shaped precipitated calcite (from bi-carbonate saturated waters) around springs and below waterfalls which dams water in pools. Inside caves it also forms around the rims of overflowing basins.

Rimstone pool: a pool formed by damming of flowing water by rimstone calcite.

Scallops: spoon-shaped hollows in a cave wall, floor, or ceiling dissolved by eddies in flowing water. Scallops are asymmetrical, with a steeper upstream end. They are usually closely packed, separated by sharp ridges. Size ranges from 10mm to 1m in length. Scallops are excellent flow indicators: the smaller they are the faster the flow; their steeper end points upstream, so that the direction of the flow in a now dry passage can be identified.

Shield: a rare cave formation consisting of two thin discs of calcite growing parallel from a cave wall fracture. As water moves under pressure out of the fracture it rapidly deposits calcite on both sides making the discs grow to one meter in diameter or even larger. The shields usually grow at a sharp angle upwards and have the rim underside often draped with stalactite.

Sinkhole: a funnel shaped enclosed hollow ranging from a few meters to several hundred meters in diameter,

formed by the solution of the substrate. Normally a sinkhole is larger than deep. When it forms by the collapse of the substrate (into a void) they can have vertical walls resembling natural shafts. Sometimes sinkholes forming in a rock substrate covered by soft, unbound sediments (alluvia) will cause the cover to subside, following the geometry of the hidden sinkholes. These are called "suffosion" sinkholes.

Soda straw: thin, hollow stalactite resembling a straw formed by the precipitation of a thin calcite film on the edges of the water drops that form at the lower end. As long as the feed is represented only by the water flowing/dripping inside the stalactite, it remains thin and of virtually the same diameter anywhere in the world (the diameter of the water drops). Once water starts flowing (as a thin film) on the outside of the stalactite, the thickness of calcite will increase and a regular stalactite forms. So in a sense a soda straw is a proto-stalactite, all stalactites starting as soda straws. The longest soda straws can reach several meters in length. This length is limited by the weight of the tube: when they become too heavy the crystalline structure breaks.

Speleothem: any kind of mineral deposits form inside caves.

Speleotherapy: treatment of certain respiratory diseases by controlled exposure to cave environment.

Stalactite: dripstone hanging from the ceiling of a cave, formed by precipitation of calcite from flowing/dripping water.

Stalagmite: dripstone growing on the floor of a cave passage by precipitation of calcite from splashing water (fed by a dripping point on the ceiling which is usually the tip of a stalactite)

Swallet (swallow hole): a place where a surface stream sinks into the ground.

Taphonomy: interdisciplinary study of processes that influence the preservation of information in the fossil record.

Troglobite: an animal that only lives in caves.

Troglophile: an animal that spends a part of its life in caves. The bat is the best representative in our times. (And maybe some of devout spelunkers....)

Trogloxene: an animal that has accidentally ended up in a cave.

Uvala: another Slovenian term describing a large, enclosed hollow that formed by the coalescing of sinkholes. Their floor is irregular usually reflecting the morphologies of the individual sinkholes.

Vadose caves: caves that formed and continue to exist mostly above the water table. The majority of their passages have air above the water.

Water budget: general quantitative accounting for water in a given hydrological cycle. In karsts, this means the amount of precipitation fallen over a karsted territory, the percentage of evaporation, the amount of runoff, the amount of sinking water and the amount of water emerging from karst outlets.

Water table: the top of a water body hosted within the sum of interconnected pores of a rock formation. In karst this means the top of the karst aquifer.

Water table caves: caves that formed in the very close to the water table, with sections formed above it (vadose) and sections formed below it (phreatic). Subsequent elevation or subsidence can change their position (turning them into full vadose or full phreatic caves), but certain morphologies may still bear witness of their original position.

INDEX

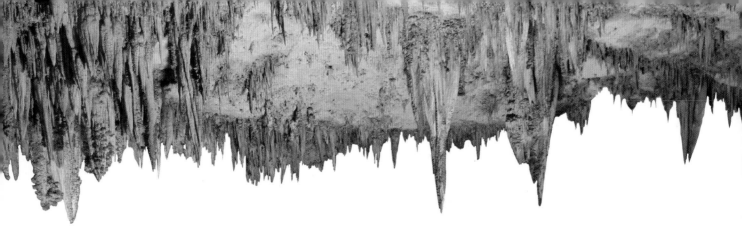

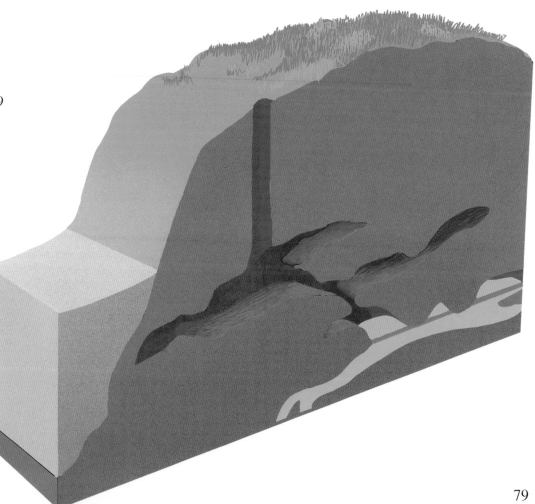

THE CAVE BOOK

Long legged whip spider

Cockroach

A cave salamander

Pseudo-scorpion

Karren at Ponoare, Mehedinti, Romania

Stalactites and stalagmites in cave

Fontaine de Fontestorbes in southern France

Polje

Natur

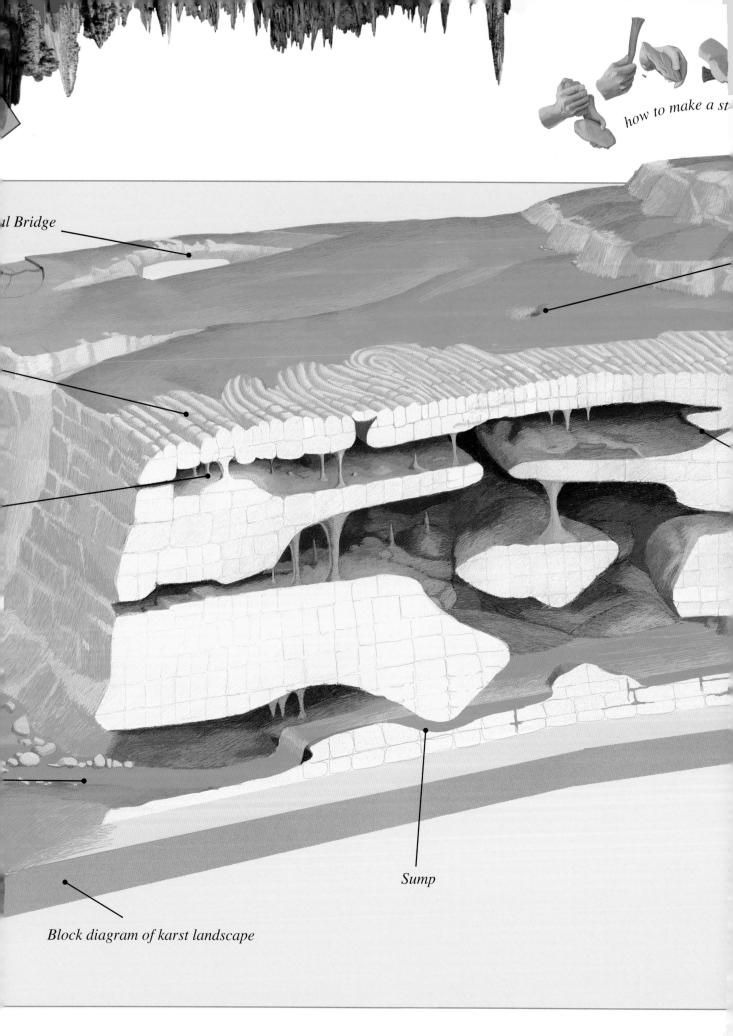

al Bridge

Sump

Block diagram of karst landscape

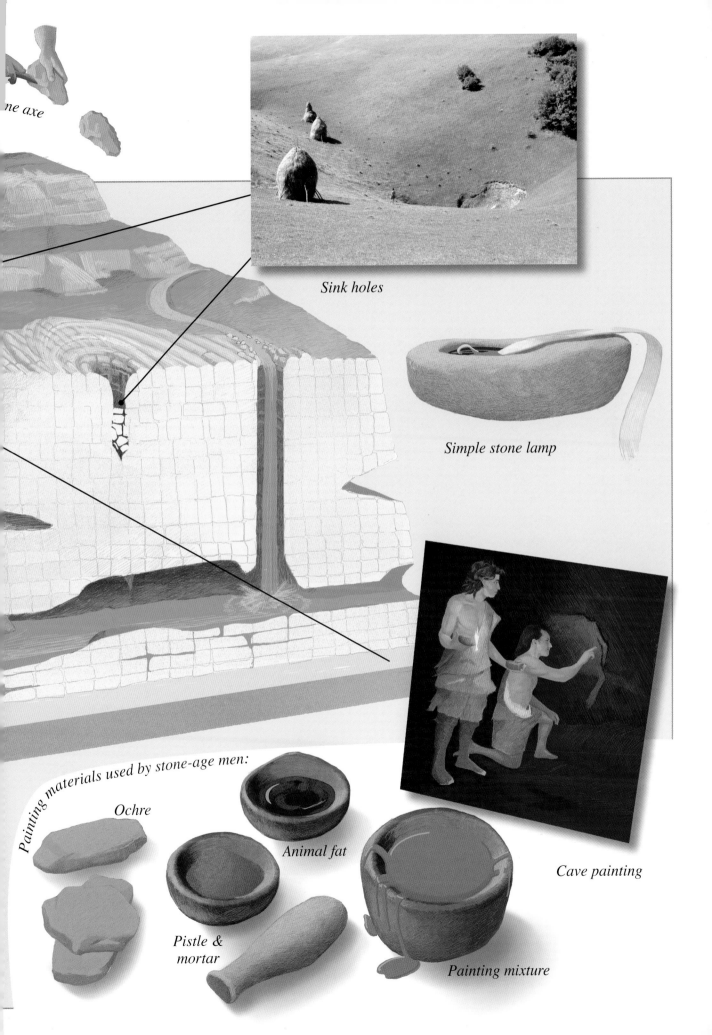

ne axe

Sink holes

Simple stone lamp

Painting materials used by stone-age men:

Ochre

Animal fat

Pistle & mortar

Painting mixture

Cave painting